The Polite Tourist

FOUR CENTURIES OF COUNTRY HOUSE VISITING

Adrian Tinniswood

The National Trust

Harry N. Abrams, Inc., Publishers

The text of this book was first published in Great Britain in 1989
by Basil Blackwell Ltd under the title *A History of Country House Visiting:
Five Centuries of Tourism and Taste*.

New edition published in 1998 by National Trust Enterprises Ltd
36 Queen Anne's Gate London SWIH 9AS

Text © Adrian Tinniswood 1989, 1998

Distributed in 1999 by Harry N. Abrams, Incorporated, New York

British Library Cataloguing in Publication Data
A catalogue record for this book is available from the British Library

ISBN 0 7078 0224 5
ISBN 0-8109-6372-8 (Abrams)

Picture research by Sophie Blair and Margaret Willes
Production by Bob Towell
Phototypeset in Adobe Caslon
by SPAN Graphics Limited, Crawley, West Sussex
Printed in Hong Kong
Phoenix Offset

Half-title: The Elysian Fields in the great landscape garden at Stowe in
Buckinghamshire. This delightful drawing by Thomas Rowlandson, dating
from about 1805, shows visitors picnicking in front of the Temple of the British
Worthies.

Frontispiece: The Lucy family in bucolic mode, showing their mansion and
estate at Charlecote Park in Warwickshire to admiring friends. This bird's-eye
view was painted by an unknown artist in 1696.

FOR

MY MOTHER

AND IN MEMORY OF

MY FATHER

Acknowledgements

Many people have helped in the writing of this book. I owe a great debt to John Hodgson for his encouragement, and for the many hours spent in his company during which he patiently helped me to develop my thoughts on the history of tourism and taste. Staff at various libraries have been unfailingly supportive, including those at the British Library, the Bodleian Library, the London Library, Cardiff City Library, and in particular Bristol Central Library. A number of friends and colleagues have taken the time to comment both on individual chapters and on the whole manuscript: my thanks to them all, and especially to Margaret Willes for her many helpful suggestions. Thanks also to Sophie Blair for her diligent picture research.

I would also like to express my gratitude to the following for permission to quote from manuscripts in their possession: Bath Reference Library; the Bodleian Library; the British Library; the Syndics of Cambridge University Library; South Glamorgan Library Authority.

Last, but by no means least, my thanks to Helen for putting up with my moods.

Contents

The First Tourists

THE ARCHITECTURAL MONUMENTS of England and Wales have been accessible to outsiders for centuries. And for centuries men and women have made special journeys to see them. Like us, they admired the image of Elizabeth I in the Long Gallery, or that portrait by Joshua Reynolds in the Drawing-Room. Like us, they raised their eyebrows at the owner's taste in furnishings, or applauded his scheme of landscape design. And like us, they often indulged in a rather vague nostalgia, or dreamed of what it must be like to live in such a place.

But there we part company from them. Wandering round Hardwick Hall or Knole, Stourhead or Petworth, our perceptions of the building, its contents, its grounds, differ fundamentally from those of the Tudor traveller or the Georgian excursionist. Our attitude towards the country house is so deeply coloured by our relationship with the past, which can never reproduce the relationship that existed between even our grandparents and history, never mind that which informed the responses of a tourist five, ten, twenty generations ago.

Take, for example, the historical framework within which medieval men and women viewed architecture. For most people in the Middle Ages, a personal awareness of the recent past was jumbled up with a multitude of myths and legends – Celtic folklore, classical learning and apocryphal Christian writings. Most chroniclers – and, as far as we know, most people who thought about British history at all – accepted that Brutus, the great-grandson of Aeneas, had arrived in Britain in 1170 BC, conquering the giants whom he found living here, and building a great city, New Troy, where London now stands. The kings of the ancient Britons, descendants of Brutus, conquered Germany and Gaul, subdued Denmark, captured and lost Rome. Julius Caesar tried to invade the country, but was repulsed, although King Arviragus was later forced to rule in co-operation with the Emperor Claudius. The Cornish King Asclepiodotus finally threw the Romans out. The Saxons arrived, to be conquered first by Aurelius Ambrosius, a Romano-Briton, and then by his nephew Arthur, who went on to defeat and rule Ireland, Iceland, the whole of Scandinavia and Gaul. Arthur then made war on Rome and an alliance of eastern kings, defeating them all and enslaving many of the Romans. He was about to take Rome itself when he was called back to Britain, wounded in a civil war and taken to the Isle of Avalon. His successors finally lost to invading hordes of Moors and Saxons, and took refuge in Cornwall and Wales, leaving the Saxons in control of most of England.

In its most basic form this was the history of Britain, as set out by the Welsh churchman Geoffrey of Monmouth in about 1135. His account, said to be taken from a newly discovered Breton chronicle of the British kings, was enormously

St James the Greater with a Donor, from a panel painting by the early fifteenth-century Flemish artist, Rogier van der Weyden, now at Petworth in Sussex. The saint is shown wearing pilgrim's garb, with his purse, staff and cockleshell badge from his shrine at Santiago de Compostela in Northern Spain. The cockleshell became the universal symbol for pilgrim travellers.

influential. It embodied existing folk-myths, a smattering of historical truth and some quite new material. But although doubts were voiced about its authenticity throughout the Middle Ages – why, for instance, did no other nation's chronicles mention Arthur as virtual emperor of northern Europe? – it was generally accepted by the vast majority, who were happy to believe that Britain had once been a great power – and would be again, according to the prophecies of Merlin as recalled by Geoffrey.

From time to time, new and often conflicting additions were made to the story. One school of thought held that Greeks who had come over with Brutus founded an academy at Oxford, which eventually, under the patronage of Alfred the Great, became the present University. Another claimed that Cambridge had been given its charter by Arthur in AD 531, and that it was a wandering group of Cambridge men who found their way to Oxford in Alfred's time and set up shop there. The monks of Glastonbury in Somerset, who claimed to have found King Arthur's tomb in the abbey grounds, decided that his mother, Igerne of Cornwall, was descended from Joseph of Arimathea and his wife, who was herself the daughter of Longinus, the spearman of the Crucifixion – who in turn was really the illegiti-mate son of Julius Caesar. Thus at one stroke Arthur's pedigree was firmly founded on the twin traditions of Christianity in its earliest stages, and Imperial Rome at its peak. The Tudor historian John Bale, Bishop of Ossory, felt that Brutus may have been fine as evidence of classical antecedents, but that a line of descent from Noah was also needed (through his grandson Samothes, first king of Britain). And Doctor Dee even suggested, in 1580, that Arthur had colonised Greenland and conquered the North Pole.

What effect such myth-making had on the ordinary person, it is hard to say. No doubt the majority believed in Brut the Trojan and Arthur, in a hazy sort of way. But whether Camelot was really Caerleon in Monmouthshire, as Gerald of Wales believed, or Cadbury in Somerset, or even Warwick (proposed by John Rous, a native of that town), depended largely on whether one had personal ties with Caerleon or Cadbury or Warwick. The important point in all this is that the medieval experience of historic architecture operated within a framework of myth and legend, some of it deliberately created for public consumption. It informed the medieval world-view, and as a result anything that pre-dated the twelfth century was interpreted in the light of a culture-set that could not distinguish between myth and history. Pre-Conquest remains were perhaps Arthurian, perhaps Roman. It didn't really matter all that much, anyway.

As far as more recent buildings were concerned, a rather different set of criteria operated. A visit to a great house usually took place for practical reasons. One went to see a relative or a friend, to do business or to cultivate an important connection. That's not to say that medieval man was blind to his surroundings, or that he lacked any ability to appreciate beauty: the concept of architecture and art as concrete expressions of function and status was familiar enough to him, and an

aesthetic response to a great house, while nowhere near as automatic as it was to become in succeeding centuries, was not unusual. And there was plenty to see. Wall decorations were common in royal palaces and noblemen's houses. There were stencilled flowers or other devices; elaborately painted wainscoting and ceilings such as that in the King's chamber at Guildford Castle, Surrey in 1256, 'of a green colour becomingly spangled with gold and silver'.[1] Ludgershall Castle in Wiltshire in 1246 had a great painting of Dives and Lazarus; the King's hall at the Palace of Clarendon, also in Wiltshire, was decorated with a Wheel of Fortune; and the early fourteenth-century Painted Chamber at Longthorpe Tower, Northamptonshire, was covered with intricate images, including the Nativity, the Seven Ages of Man and the Wheel of the Five Senses. Most of the more sophisticated murals had a moral or religious rather than a purely aesthetic purpose; but they were still meant to be *seen* by favoured guests. Henry II's chamber at Winchester Castle was painted with a representation of an eagle being savaged by its four offspring, an obvious reference to the King's problems with his own four sons, and one that was clearly intended to provoke comment from visitors.

Such things were part and parcel of the display of greatness which supported and confirmed a king's or nobleman's position. But few people actually sought to gain access to them solely for the purpose of seeing art-objects as such. The foreign diplomat admitted to the king's presence and the aristocratic recipient of a nobleman's hospitality certainly admired the trappings of wealth. But that admiration was almost always ancillary to the main object of a visit.

Perhaps the true ancestor of the tourist was neither the lord, moving with his cumbersome entourage from house to house, nor the chronicler, with his mixture of fact, fable and fantasy. It was the pilgrim. The cult of pilgrimage reached an astonishing peak during the Middle Ages: at the height of its popularity 500,000 people a year came from all over Europe to visit the shrine of the Apostle James the Greater at Santiago de Compostela in Northern Spain. Guidebooks and foreign-language phrase-books were available for pilgrims to Rome and the Holy Land. And even in England, which couldn't compete with Rome, Jerusalem or Compostela, some 200,000 travellers a year came to St Thomas Becket's shrine at Canterbury. At the beginning of the sixteenth century Erasmus wrote that the Norfolk town of Walsingham, where the heavenly milk of the Virgin was preserved, 'is maintained by scarcely anything else but the number of its visitors'.[2]

The motives of such visitors were mixed. Predominant among them was the idea of fulfilling a vow made in time of crisis; or doing penance; or obtaining indulgences – partial or total relief from Purgatory – for one's dead friends or relatives. Indulgences were often a powerful incentive to visit, and shrines that had fallen on hard times could benefit from papal grants of this facility. At Hailes Abbey in Gloucestershire, for example, where the major attraction was a phial of Christ's blood, a pronouncement by scholastic philosophers that all such relics must be fakes (since any blood that Christ had shed must have been reunited with his body at the Resurrection) caused a serious fall-off in attendances at the shrine.

Hailes Abbey in Gloucestershire, from an eighteenth-century watercolour by the Bath artist, Thomas Robins the Elder. In the Middle Ages, Hailes was one of the great pilgrimage centres in England, attracting large numbers of travellers with its phial of Christ's blood.

It was only when a series of fifteenth-century popes granted indulgences to those who worshipped at Hailes that the Abbey's fortunes took a turn for the better.

Inevitably, more secular motives blended in with the religious, and exemption from taxes, the exhilaration of seeing a famous shrine and the consequent enhancement of status within one's community must all have played their part. So too did the pleasure of participating in a communal leisure activity: Mary, daughter of Edward I, was a rather reluctant nun, whose frequent pilgrimages offered a welcome diversion from life in the convent. On one occasion she lost so much money dicing that she had to borrow from her servants.

The blend of recreation and genuine piety which characterised many medieval pilgrimages is not the only thing that points to the pilgrim as the ancestor of the modern tourist. The exotic nature of the destination, and the social structures which grew up around it to cater for large numbers of visitors, both serve as indicators of the shape of things to come. So too does the sheer spectacle which greeted the pilgrim: the bones of saints were housed in feretories decorated with gold, ivory, silver or silver-gilt, encrusted with diamonds, rubies and other gems; the heads in *chefs*, small coffers often depicting the saint's face as the craftsman imagined it; the arms in arm-shaped cases; and the other bits and pieces in chests of gold and crystal, or ivory.

The actual mechanics of visiting a great shrine are described in detail by Erasmus. In 1510 he and his companions visited Canterbury. The cathedral had been venerated as the shrine of a number of saints for several centuries before the death of its most famous archbishop, Becket, whose savage murder at the end of December 1170 assured it of its place as a major European centre of pilgrimage. Having seen Becket's clothes, and an assortment of jaw-bones, teeth, hands, arms and fingers, the exhibition of which 'seemed likely to last for ever, if my sometime unmanageable companion had not interrupted the zeal of the showman', Erasmus was taken into a chapel where Becket's body lay: 'A wooden canopy covers the shrine, and when that is drawn up with ropes, inestimable treasures are opened to view. The least valuable part is gold; every part glistened, shone, and sparkled with rare and very large jewels, some of them exceeding the size of a goose's egg.' When they had finished praying, the attendant 'with a white wand pointed out each jewel, telling its name in French, its value, and the name of its donor'.[3] Erasmus was certainly no friend to the Church, and his cynicism echoes the contempt with which Protestants and humanists alike were to regard the practice of pilgrimage. Yet his descriptions ring true, and one can see in the well-co-ordinated spectacle he depicts a blend of piety and showmanship which must have excited most medieval pilgrims.

The organisation of pilgrimage as a structured leisure activity, with its exploitation as a revenue-earner, and the various sites vying with each other to attract ever larger numbers of visitors, obviously has its parallels in the tourist industry of today. And those parallels can be carried further. A superstructure of peripheral amenities grew up around each shrine – stalls, street vendors, souvenir-sellers, inns and lodging-houses, all dependent on the visitor. Wandering round the secluded ruins of Hailes Abbey today, we might imagine the monks and devout pilgrims worshipping the phial of holy blood which drew so many to the spot. What is harder to imagine is the mass of service industries which existed to cater for those visitors. It is perhaps no exaggeration to say that never again, until the rapid growth in twentieth-century tourism, would there be such an extensive network of social structures devoted to catering for and exploiting one particular category of traveller.

It would be easy to take the image of the pilgrim-as-tourist too far, to concentrate on the externals of medieval pilgrimage whilst glossing over its religious significance. But, in a sense, it is the externals that concern us. They show a widespread social activity which laid down a pattern of behaviour that tourists were to follow. With the dissolution of the monasteries and the destruction of shrines which ensued during the middle years of the sixteenth century, this activity came to an abrupt halt. Relics were destroyed; the institutions that maintained them were swept away; and in the royal palaces and aristocratic mansions that remained, the wealthy, at least, found new places to visit, new secular shrines at which to worship. Slowly, but surely, the trappings of power would become as legitimate an object of interest as the fragments of bone and wood and cloth before which their grandparents had knelt and prayed.

Lead pilgrimage badges found in archaeological digs in London. The badges at the bottom were given to those who made the pilgrimage to the tomb of St Thomas Becket in Canterbury Cathedral.

CHAPTER I

Built For Envious Show

> We then went on into the nearby palace, the royal residence
> known as Whitehall, ie the White Hall. It is truly majestic . . .
> and it is a place which fills one with wonder, not so much
> because of its great size as because of the magnificence of its
> bed chambers and living rooms which are filled with the most
> gorgeous splendour.
>
> *The Diary of Baron Waldstein*, 1600[1]

SOCIAL STRUCTURES were altering radically in late sixteenth-century England. A new landed class was emerging, typified by men like Edward Phelips, the ambitious lawyer and builder of Montacute in Somerset; Sir Francis Willoughby, the shrewd industrialist who commissioned Robert Smythson to create a flamboyant hilltop palace at Wollaton in Nottinghamshire; and Sir William Sharington, a shady and unscrupulous financier who bought and converted the former Augustinian nunnery at Lacock in Wiltshire.

These men had much stronger links with business than did the medieval landed elites. A survey of the owners of country estates in Hertfordshire shows a steep increase in the proportion of owners with commercial connections during the later sixteenth and early seventeenth centuries, rising from around 1 in 5 among those born in the 1550s, to 1 in 2.5 of those born in the early 1600s.[2] And such men replaced, or at least supplemented, the traditional nobleman with his vast, quasi-military entourage and his highly localised powerbase. Although he did not disappear from the scene entirely, the Elizabethan emphasis on a stronger central government based around the Court and the law courts meant that his days were numbered.

Since it was the new class of entrepreneurs who were the major builders at this time, men anxious to consolidate their social position, still able to remember their relatively humble roots and still insecure enough to try to distance themselves from them, it is scarcely surprising that the country houses of the period are characterised by a triumph of form over function. Discussing the links between building and status, Francis Bacon wrote that 'when men sought to cure mortality by fame . . . buildings were the only way'.[3] William Camden commended the siting of the Countess of Shrewsbury's two houses, the Old and New Halls at Hardwick in Derbyshire, 'which by reason of their lofty situation show themselves, a far off to be seen'.[4] Hardwick and Wollaton and Montacute, towering over the landscape,

Sir Edward Phelips, the lawyer who built Montacute House in Somerset. This portrait by an unknown artist shows Phelips with his mace and seal bag as Speaker of the House of Commons, standing in front of the armorial stained glass in the window of his Great Chamber at Montacute. The statement is clear – this is a man of property with powerful allies at court and in the county.

Lacock Abbey in Wiltshire, an Augustinian nunnery that was converted into a private house at the Dissolution by Sir William Sharington, one of the 'new men' of the Tudor court. In the foreground is the octagonal tower that he built in the Renaissance style, in contrast to the Gothic cloisters (*right*) which he retained from the monastic house.

demanding attention and admiration, were clear pointers to the rage to advertise one's wealth and status.

But the desire to impress and to display presupposes an audience, and the scale of the new elite's prodigy houses was clearly intended to attract the notice and respect of more than just the tenantry and immediate neighbours, important though that function might be. For the Court circle, a primary objective was certainly a visit from Queen Elizabeth herself, with all of the opportunities for

The Long Gallery at Montacute runs
right across the top of the house,
ending in spectacular bow windows
that resemble an Elizabethan galleon.

preferment and perquisites which that might bring. Indeed, William Cecil's
Burghley in Northamptonshire, Theobalds in Hertfordshire, where Cecil built
one of the most spectacular houses of the age, and Sir Christopher Hatton's vast
palace at Holdenby in Northamptonshire, were much more than private country
houses: they were intended to flatter and honour Elizabeth. She came thirteen
times to Theobalds, making it, in effect, another royal palace. As Cecil cynically
remarked to Hatton in 1579 apropos their building schemes, 'God send us both
long to enjoy her for whom we both meant to exceed our purses in these'.[5] Hatton
was more deferential: he rarely visited Holdenby, confessing to Sir Thomas
Heneage in September 1580 that he meant to leave this 'shrine, I mean Holdenby,
still unseen until that holy saint may sit in it, to whom it is dedicated'.[6]

However, if Hatton was reluctant to visit his new 'shrine' until it was occupied
by his sovereign, others were not. In 1581 Barnaby Rich was commenting that
'many gentlemen and strangers that come but to see the house are there daily
welcomed, feasted, and well lodged'.[7] There is clear evidence that such major
building schemes attracted a great deal of interest among the nobility and gentry.
We can see in Rich's statement an indication of a transitional phase between the
medieval business of the country house as a provider of hospitality and its more
recent function as a place to be visited for its curiosity value.

The combination of the two roles, guest and tourist, was occasionally supplemented by a third: that of the amateur and critic. It was quite common for an
aristocrat engaged in a major building project not only to send his mason or
surveyor to see other new or partially completed houses, but to go himself – or
herself, in the case of the Dowager Countess of Shrewsbury, who in the late
summer of 1592, when her new residence at Hardwick was in the early stages of
construction, visited both Holdenby and Wollaton.

Where interested social equals were concerned, plans were exchanged, and
advice and criticism sought and received. The courtier Sir Ralph Sadleir, whose
London residence was Sutton House in Hackney, called in to see the still incom-
plete Burghley on his way to Scotland in the summer of 1559. He wrote to tell Cecil
that 'I like what is done, and the order of the rest as your man showed it cannot but
be fair. God send you money enough to end it with; other lack I see none.'[8] And in
a letter to Cecil dated 9 August 1579, Hatton expressly invited his criticisms of
Holdenby, showing at the same time how he had been inspired by the latter's
Hertfordshire house: 'For as the same is done hitherto in direct observation of
your house and plots of Theobalds, so I earnestly pray your Lordship that by your
good corrections at this time, it may appear as like to the same as it hath ever been
meant to be.'[9] Cecil was impressed, as he wrote to Hatton after his visit:

> [A]pproaching to the house, being led by a large, long, straight fair way, I
> found a great magnificence in the front or front pieces of the house, and so
> every part answerable to other, to allure liking. I found no one thing of
> greater grace than your stately ascent from your hall to your great chamber,

and your chamber answerable with largeness and lightsomeness, that truly a Momus could find no fault. I visited all your rooms, high and low, and only the contentation of mine eyes made me forget the infirmity of my legs.[10]

As we have seen, both Holdenby and Theobalds were built for the reception of the Queen, and during her reign Elizabeth ranks as the most important – and one of the most dedicated – of country-house visitors. As soon as she was crowned, she began a series of extended summer tours around the southern and middle parts of her realm. These annual progresses grew out of medieval practice – the great lord moving with his household from one estate to another – but they became essentially political manoeuvres designed to enhance her public image, to promote goodwill and to foster stronger links with her subjects. Her itineraries varied enormously. Some were little more than short excursions out of the capital, while others were major expeditions into the provinces. But no matter how limited or extensive their scope, the select few who were chosen to play host to their monarch could not afford to spare any expense for her entertainment and pleasure.

The inconvenience of a royal visit was often considerable. Accommodation had to be found not only for the Queen and her personal attendants, but also for large numbers of government officials – and their servants. When the Queen visited Theobalds in 1583, for example, perhaps as many as 150 people had to be housed: Cecil had to move his table from the great chamber; his steward gave up his lodgings to the royal plate; and his servants ate in the joiners' workshop and slept on pallets in a converted storehouse. In effect, the house became a temporary royal palace, with one important difference – Cecil had to foot the bill. Each royal visit to Theobalds cost Elizabeth's Lord High Treasurer between two and three thousand pounds, 'the Queen lying there at his lordship's charge sometimes three weeks or a month, or six weeks together'. Ambassadors would visit her, to be received in full state, and there were 'rich shows, pleasant devices, and all manner of sports that could be devised, to the great delight of her Majesty and her whole train'.[11]

Theobalds was exceptional, in that Elizabeth visited no other country house so frequently, and rarely stayed so long. A night or two was the norm, but, even so, she expected the lavish entertainments and extravagant displays of loyalty which befitted the reception of a monarch elevated by state policy almost to the status of demi-goddess. When she visited Osterley in Middlesex, the home of the builder of the Royal Exchange, Sir Thomas Gresham, in the late 1570s, she happened to mention that the central courtyard was too big, and that it might be improved if it were divided in two: 'What doth Sir Thomas, but in the night time sends for workmen to London (money commands all things), who so speedily and silently apply their business, that the next morning discovered the court double, which the night had left single before.'[12] One suspects that this anecdote suffers a little from Elizabethan hyperbole: it is hard to believe that any workman could erect a wall

Elizabeth I, a portrait painted by Nicholas Hilliard and Rowland Lockey for Bess of Hardwick in the 1590s, still hanging in the Long Gallery at Hardwick. The Queen is shown almost as an impersonal image, the approved style of portraiture for her as she grew older and the cult of the goddess grew stronger.

overnight without rousing the entire household. But the Queen was said to be both pleased and surprised, while her courtiers used Gresham's display as an excuse for some rather laboured wit, 'some avowing it was no wonder he could so soon *change a building*, who could *build a change*'; others, referring to some family problems which Gresham was having, 'affirmed that a house is easier divided than united'.[13]

By ensuring that Elizabeth had a pleasing stay at his house, the Tudor nobleman not only emphasised his loyalty and obedience to the Crown, but also put himself in the way of those favours which might double his income overnight. But the Queen could be a demanding guest, as her visit to Sir John Puckering at Kew demonstrates only too clearly. Sir John, who had recently obtained a perk worth some £100 a year, was anxious to show his gratitude. As soon as Elizabeth arrived she was given a diamond-encrusted fan. Between the garden gate and the house she was met by a servant with a speech of greeting and a bouquet containing 'a very rich jewel, with pendants of unfurled diamonds, valued at £400 at least'. After eating, in her privy chamber Sir John presented her with a pair of virginals; in her bed-chamber he gave her a fine gown. One might think that such a dazzling array of gifts would be enough; however, after all this, 'to grace his lordship the more, she of herself took from him a salt, a spoon, and a fork, of fair agate'.[14] It was obviously prudent to lock up the cutlery when Elizabeth came to visit.

Queen Elizabeth, although the most illustrious of 'tourists' during the period covered by this chapter, was not the only country-house visitor. Some, to whom we shall return later, were close kin to tourists in the modern sense of the word, but a brief mention at least must be made of another group who were engaged in systematic explorations of the history and antiquities of their country. These were the mapmakers and geographers, chroniclers and antiquaries – men like John Dee and John Stowe and John Speed, Humphrey Lluyd and William Harrison, Ralph Holinshed and Richard Carew – all struggling to create an image of Britain and to pass on their discoveries to their fellows in the flood of topographical publications which appeared during Elizabeth's reign.

The reasons for this new interest in the nation's history and geography are diverse and complex, but chief among them was the need to legitimise the new post-Reformation course which England was taking, independently from many of its neighbours. A number of Protestant scholars and historians were seeking to discover or even to manufacture a national identity almost as an act of solidarity, by drawing together past and present into a single assimilable whole, giving a shape to what had previously been little more than a loose, imperfectly perceived collection of settlements, monuments and anecdotes.

The first of these Tudor topographers and antiquaries was John Leland (1503–52). Having been given a warrant by Henry VIII 'to peruse and diligently to search all the libraries of monasteries and colleges of this your noble realm, to the intent that the monuments of ancient writers as well of other nations, as of this your own province might be brought out of deadly darkness to lively light',[15]

Leland was inspired to visit and record the places of which he had read. In the words of his New Year's gift to the King in 1546, he was:

> totally inflamed with a love to see thoroughly all those parts of this your opulent and ample realm that I had read of in the aforesaid writers. In so much that all my other occupations intermitted, I have so travelled in your dominions both by the sea coasts and the middle parts, sparing neither labour nor costs by the space of these six years past, that there is almost neither cape nor bay, haven, creek or pier, river or confluence of rivers, breaches, washes, lakes, meres, fenny waters, mountains, valleys, moors, heaths, forests, woods, cities, boroughs, castles, principal manor places, monasteries, and colleges, but I have seen them, and noted in so doing a whole world of things very memorable.[16]

His intention was to make a great map of England and Wales, and to write the first detailed topographical description of them – a monumental task, but one that would have gone a long way towards shaping a cohesive national consciousness.

Given the scope of Leland's proposed work, it is scarcely surprising that he provides little in the way of detailed architectural description. His account of Denbigh Castle in Wales is lengthier than most:

> The castle is a very large thing, and hath many towers in it. But the body of the work was never finished. The gate house is a marvellous strong and great piece of work, but the *fastigia* of it were never finished. If they had been, it might have been counted among the most memorable pieces of works in England [*sic*]. It hath divers wards and divers portcullisses.[17]

Strength and size are the keynotes in an account of military architecture, and it would be unfair to criticise Leland for superficiality: the vocabulary necessary for critical analysis hardly existed in his day (although it would soon appear), and, in any case, his purpose was to record rather than to evaluate. Rarely does he describe interiors, although he does say of Ewelme Manor, near Wallingford in Oxfordshire, that 'the hall of it is fair and hath great bars of iron . . . instead of cross beams. The parlour by is exceeding fair and lightsome: and so be all the lodgings there.'[18] Occasionally, however, he does express a hint of a more thoroughgoing antiquarian appreciation of the monuments to the past, as in his remarks on Sudeley Castle in Gloucestershire, which 'goeth to ruin, more pity'.[19]

In the event, Leland was prevented from achieving his aim of publishing a nation-wide survey – by 'a most pitiful occasion he fell besides his wits', in the words of a friend, and he died insane in 1552. But his researches, which circulated in manuscript form, laid the foundations on which others were to build. County surveys, beginning with Lambarde's *Perambulation of Kent* (1576), and continuing with Richard Carew's delightful *Survey of Cornwall* (published in 1602, but written in the 1590s) and George Owen's *Description of Pembrokeshire* (1603), showed that an increasing number of scholars were touring the countryside, voraciously recording, collecting and interpreting all that they saw – industries, natural phenomena and architectural monuments and remains.

The most famous of these new topographers, after Leland, was one who attracted the praise of both Edmund Spenser –

> Camden! the nurse of antiquity,
> And lantern unto late succeeding age,
> To see the light of simple verity
> Buried in ruins . . .
> Camden! though Time all monuments obscure,
> Yet thy just labours ever shall endure.[20]

– and Ben Jonson:

> Camden, most reverend head, to whom I owe
> All that I am in arts, all that I know . . .
> What name, what skill, what faith hath thou in things!
> What sight in searching the most antique springs!
> What weight, and what authority in thy speech![21]

William Camden (1551–1623) was a thirty-five-year-old schoolmaster at Westminster when the first edition of his *Britannia* was published in 1586. The book is hard to discuss as a single entity, not least because it developed from a small octavo volume to a massive, copiously illustrated folio consisting of some 860 pages when the author, who became Clarenceaux Herald in the College of Arms in 1597, was enabled by his new job to spend even more time in touring the country. It is wide-ranging in its aims and in its achievements; in Camden's own words, his intentions were: 'In each county . . . to describe its ancient inhabitants, etymology of its name, its limits, soil, remarkable places both ancient and modern, and its dukes or earls from the Norman Conquest.'[22] His descriptions are, like Leland's, brief, informative, factual and wide-ranging, from the iron-works in Birmingham, through the prospects from Windsor Castle and Hardwick Hall, to the Roman Camp at Ambleside in the Lake District and King John's Cup at King's Lynn in Norfolk. But Camden's importance – and the importance of his fellow-scholars – for a study of tourism and popular perceptions of architecture lies not so much in what he said, or even in his attitudes towards past and present building, as in the fact that, unlike previous writers, he actually went to *see* so many of the things which he described. Certainly he borrowed from others, and recorded hearsay and rumour; but, together with a team of like-minded friends, Camden did tour large areas of Britain, and his researches, like those of Leland, not only fostered a notion of the value of the remains of the past, but also helped to encourage succeeding generations to leave their firesides and to explore their country for themselves.

Another, more clearly defined group of explorers touring England and Wales in the late sixteenth and early seventeenth centuries were foreigners, mainly from the

Ann° dñi. 1586

Ætatis suæ. 32.

Chi verace durera.

Sir Richard Carew, author of the *Survey of Cornwall*, published in 1602. In this book he reveals himself not only as a scholar, fascinated by the minutiae of life, but a humane individual at peace with himself, finding particular pleasure in his 'fishful pond' at his home in Antony.

The Great Picture of the Clifford family, commissioned by Lady Anne Clifford in 1646 when at last she came into her rightful inheritance in the north of England. This detail shows her as a fifteen-year-old girl, in 1605, with portraits of her tutor and governess, and the books that she had in her youth. These include Gerard's *Herball*, Sir Philip Sidney's *Arcadia*, all of the works of Chaucer and Spenser, and, prominently displayed on the floor, Camden's *Britannia*.

Protestant states of Germany and Middle Europe. They were young men, mostly – the discomforts of long-distance travel were not for the elderly – and they came either on diplomatic or quasi-diplomatic missions, or as part of a general 'Grand Tour' of Europe, completing their education in much the same way that the English aristocrat would travel to France and Italy one hundred years later.

For such visitors, a clear pattern of travel had already emerged by the 1580s: a crossing from Calais or Boulogne to Dover, usually in August or September; post-horses to Canterbury (with perhaps a quick visit to the Cathedral), Sittingbourne, Rochester and Gravesend; and then by boat along the Thames to London – 2d for a place on the common barge, which sailed on every tide, and 6d for a seat in the tiltboat. In the capital the tourist and his entourage would set up base in one of the inns which specialised in catering for foreigners – the White Bear, perhaps, or the Black Bell, or Monsieur Briard's Fleur de Lys in Mark Lane.

Such an itinerary sounds straightforward. In fact, it was beset with dangers and difficulties, beginning with the Channel crossing itself. The experience of Duke Frederick of Würtemberg's party, who sailed from Emden in August 1592, was typical: 'Not being accustomed to the sea, we were seized by horrible vomitings, and most of our party (with the exception of his Highness) became so dreadfully ill that they thought they were dying.'[23] The eighteen-year-old Moravian Baron Waldstein suffered a similar fate on his return journey from Dover to Boulogne, but described his experience rather less melodramatically: a plaintive note scrawled in the margin of his diary on 6 August 1600 simply records 'I was seasick'.[24]

Nor did the foreigner's trials and tribulations end at Dover. If he didn't possess the necessary credentials, he might be kept waiting for several days while his name was cleared by government officials in London. (Waldstein was told by the Port Authorities that he would not be allowed into the country until his name had been submitted to the Queen, because of a security scare caused by the arrival at one of the royal palaces of three Austrians, who looked round the kitchens and then bolted, obviously giving rise to suspicions about poisoning Elizabeth.) When the traveller was finally allowed to move up through Kent, the strangeness of the English saddle could make the ride by post-horse an unpleasant experience, as reported by Jacob Rathgeb, the Duke of Würtemberg's private secretary:

> Some of the party did not feel themselves quite at ease, particularly his Highness, on account of the saddles being in these parts so small and covered only with bare hide or leather, and therefore painful and hard to ride upon, and it is difficult, especially for any one who is corpulent and heavy, to settle himself comfortably on such small saddles.[25]

Although most tourists put up with the discomfort, one at least gave up at Canterbury, and went in search of a coach for the rest of the journey. Thomas Platter, touring in 1599, remarked on his companions' 'great discomfort from the posts because of the small saddles which they had to ride without post cushions', and

Far left: The Old and New Halls at Hardwick in Derbyshire. In the foreground is the Old Hall, Bess's birthplace which she refurbished in the 1580s. In the background is the New Hall, begun in 1590 at the death of her husband, Lord Shrewsbury. To ensure that all who saw the house should know who had created it, and her status, Bess surmounted the towers with her initials and countess's coronet (*left*).

went on to describe the five-horse wagon which they hired, and which had 'like all such wagons in England only two wheels, yet they hold as much as do our coaches abroad, for they are very long'.[26]

Safely ensconced in London, the tourist had now to arrange for a guide and interpreter to show him the sights, especially if he planned to make an extended tour. Aids to overcoming the language barrier were being published as early as the 1580s, in the form of tourists' phrase-books. They contained little incidents with scenes which the foreign traveller might meet on his journey, including the following account of how to communicate with a chambermaid:

TRAVELLER: My shee frinde, is my bed made? is it good?
JOAN: Yea Sir, it is a good federbed, the scheetes be very cleane.
TRAVELLER: Pull of my hosen and Warme my bed: drawe the curtines, and pin them with a pin. My shee frinde, kiss me once, and I shall sleape the better. I thanke you fayre mayden.[27]

And on leaving, the traveller is shown the correct procedure with regard to tipping: 'Where is ye mayden? hold my shee freend, ther is for your paines.' One can only marvel at the thought of the Duke of Würtemberg, or Baron Waldstein, phrase-book in one hand and chambermaid in the other, making advances to his 'shee frinde' in halting English.

The dialogue quoted above comes from a set of parallel texts in Flemish, English, German, Latin, Italian, Spanish and French, and such multi-lingual manuals were evidently popular, with new editions appearing regularly. In any case, most tourists would be able to communicate with educated English men and women fairly happily in what was at that time an international language. In 1616 Justus Zinzerling noted that the inn-keeper at Sittingbourne was 'a Scotchman, a very good man, and knows Latin'.[28] And the young Baron Waldstein, presented to Elizabeth I at Greenwich in the course of his 1600 tour, made an elaborate speech to her in Latin. Wandering around the country lanes of Oxfordshire two years later, and separated from the rest of their party, Frederick Gerschow and Joachim Tribsees had cause to be thankful for their knowledge of the language:

> A gentleman noticing us from afar, and easily recognising us to be foreigners who had got off the right road, rode up to us, and asked in Latin where we wished to go to . . .
>
> When, at last, we reached an inn, we could not, for want of an interpreter, get anything to eat or drink, until Frederick Gerschow found a learned parson in the village, who procured everything we wanted, and even, for a short time, left some of his own guests whom he had invited on that evening to settle accounts with the landlord, and thus showed us great honour and kindness. That day I would not have missed knowing Latin for a thaler.[29]

But most foreign sightseers would prefer to hire their own interpreter, and it is some indication of the growth in tourism during the period that by the later sixteenth century, mechanisms for doing so were already well established. For those in search of a German-speaking guide, the Steelyard in Lower Thames Street – a branch of the Hanseatic League, also called the 'German House' – was one obvious source. It was here that Lupold von Wedel, a Pomeranian soldier of fortune, found his interpreter, John Wachendorf. Another well-known interpreter was one Linyard or Leinvert, a 'German tailor who acts as a guide to persons of our nation, and knows a good deal about the country'.[30] But there were others elsewhere, relying on personal recommendation and word of mouth for their business, some trustworthy, others less so. Justus Zinzerling, a Thuringian Doctor of Law whose published travels in Europe became a standard guide, gives the following advice in the 1616 edition of his *Itineris Anglici verbissima delineatio*:

> Those who are desirous of visiting the entire kingdom hire interpreters, of whom there are many who make it a profession. Not a few Germans have complained of the deceit of these fellows; we employed a most excellent

youth named Frederick, a native of Hesse Cassel, who may be heard of at the sign of the Black Bell . . . which is recommended as a good economical establishment.[31]

Once settled in London, and with a guide-interpreter in tow, the tour tended to follow an established pattern. Several days would be spent in the capital itself, with the traveller seeing the sights while horses were hired and arrangements made for the extended tour. With that peculiar blend of barbarism and culture which typified Elizabethan England (and, no doubt, the rest of Europe), the theatre was usually on the agenda, together with cock-fighting, bull-baiting and bear-baiting. In spite of the problems posed by the difference in language (one wonders if the guide gave a running commentary), the theatre was popular with most of the foreign tourists who have left accounts of their time in England. Detailed descriptions of either the theatre or the play are rarely given ('In the afternoon a tragic play was acted about Samson and the half tribe of Benjamin', writes Frederick Gerschow[32]); but often the traveller gives us just enough to make us want to hear more. In an entry in his diary for Monday, 3 July 1600, Waldstein records that he 'went to see an English play. The theatre follows the ancient Roman plan: it is built of wood and is so designed that the spectators can get a comfortable view of everything that happens in any part of the building.'[33] This may be a description of the Globe, scarcely a year old – but it might equally well be the Rose, or the Swan. Other tourists are more specific. On Monday, 30 April 1610, Lewis Frederick of Würtemberg 'went to the Globe, the usual place for acting plays; the history of the Moor of Venice was represented there'.[34] Eleven years earlier, Thomas Platter had crossed the Thames and 'there in the house with the thatched roof witnessed an excellent performance of the tragedy of the first Emperor Julius Caesar with a cast of some fifteen people'.[35] Unfortunately, neither Lewis Frederick nor Platter has anything to say about the quality of, or reception given to *Othello* or *Julius Caesar*. It would be nice to think that they enjoyed the performance.

But the various entertainments which London had to offer were ancillary to the main aims of any foreign visitor's expedition to England. First, he came to see – and if possible to have an audience with – the monarch.

Responses to Elizabeth varied. The middle-aged soldier of Protestantism, Lupold von Wedel, was obviously impressed at the sight of the Queen as she entered London in November 1584. She 'sat in an open gilt carriage under a canopy of red velvet, embroidered with gold and pearls', and 'looked like goddesses are wont to be painted'.[36] Von Wedel was witnessing the cult of Elizabeth in action. Waldstein, on the other hand, who was presented to her at Greenwich sixteen years later, actively contributed to the cult in his speech, telling Elizabeth that 'I shall not cease from devoting myself to proclaiming, wheresoever I find myself, the extreme goodness of Your Majesty to me, so that the whole world may know

The High Great Chamber at Hardwick, one of the state apartments that Bess built on the top floor. She lived in the hope that Queen Elizabeth might pay a visit to the house, and the apartments were furnished ready for such an occasion. The plaster frieze above the tapestries represents the court of Diana the virgin goddess and huntress, an allusion to Elizabeth, the Virgin Queen. Diana herself is depicted directly above the chairs of state under their canopy – this is where Bess would have received her visitors.

the adoration with which I look up to, revere, and worship Your Majesty, as some goddess come down from the skies.'[37]

The references to the Queen as goddess reinforce the powerful image promulgated by Elizabeth's ministers and demonstrate one of the reasons, perhaps, for the eagerness of the German Protestant nobility to visit England. She was Diana, she was Astarte – although the eighteen-year-old Waldstein, faced with a gaunt, haggard and elderly woman, was honest enough to admit that the 'beauty and shapeliness' of her maids of honour 'had no difficulty in diverting the eyes and minds of some of the spectators'.[38]

For a slightly less reverent picture we must turn to the young Duke of Pomerania-Wolgast, who saw Elizabeth in September 1602, just six months before her death. His secretary and diarist, Frederick Gerschow, managed – presumably with the Duke's approval – to deliver the most back-handed of compliments: having noted that the Queen's portraits showed that she must have been a great beauty in her youth, he coolly observed that 'even in her old age she did not look ugly, when seen from a distance'.[39]

When one comes to examine the foreign visitor's reaction to the architecture of the palaces which formed a well-defined tour by the end of the sixteenth century, two things quickly become clear: the surprising sophistication of the mechanisms already in operation at these royal palaces; and the undiscriminating nature of the tourist's response. He was emphatically not a connoisseur, passing informed and critical judgements on what he saw – he was a sightseer, eager to take in anything of interest, from buildings to paintings to curiosities of all kinds, from elaborate fountains and furnishings to 'a cow with six legs' and 'a round horn which had grown on an English woman's forehead'.[40]

In the royal palaces at least, staff were not only attendants in the traditional sense, but also functioned as guides (and security men) and obtained revenue from that role. Tourists consistently talk of being 'shown around' various rooms at Whitehall, Windsor, Hampton Court and so on; they mention particular items which are brought out and, again, 'shown' to them; and Thomas Platter makes it clear that it is the household servants, rather than the German interpreters accompanying the visitors, who are doing the showing. Talking of his visit to Nonsuch in Surrey in 1599, he mentions that Lord Cobham 'put us in charge of someone to guide us over the palace'; while at Hampton Court, he is shown round the interior by one guide, and then handed on to a gardener, who 'conducted us into the royal pleasaunce'.[41] And John Donne describes the activities of the verger at Westminster Abbey, the man

> . . . that keeps the Abbey tombs
> And for his price doth with whoever comes
> Of all our Harrys and our Edwards talk.[42]

However, at Westminster, from 1600 onwards at least, the visitor had the benefit of one of the earliest of guidebooks, Camden's account of the inscriptions. 'The

Abbey', says Waldstein, 'contains a large number of chapels and some very splendid royal monuments: with reference to these, consult a special book, which is
printed in London.' Epitaphs and inscriptions 'are given in a little book', says
Frederick Gerschow two years later; and Justus Zinzerling recommends 'a printed
book of the monuments [which] is sold by the verger'.[43] It went through at least
three editions in six years, and, quite apart from his other contributions to topo-
graphy and antiquarianism, Camden deserves a place in the history of tourism as
the author of one of the earliest English site-specific guidebooks.

The practice of paying for admission and information, if only on an unregulated,

informal basis, was also an integral part of a visit to the palaces, even at this early date. Zinzerling, describing a visit to the Paradise Room at Hampton Court in his *Itineris Anglici verbissima delineatio*, remarked: 'It is strange that the keeper of this room is so sordid that you must bargain with him beforehand about his fee; yet from his dress he appears a grand gentleman'.[44] And Thomas Platter became steadily more exasperated during his tour of the Tower of London: in the armoury 'we made the first gratuity to a keeper in attendance, 3 English shillings'; further on, 'we gave largesse for the third time'; on being shown a 'very ancient tapestry which had been in this castle some five hundred years . . . we gave the fifth gratuity';

A painting of Greenwich Palace, probably a copy of a lost picture by Cornelis Bol, a topographical artist who worked in London in the 1630s. It contains the most complete depiction of Henry VIII's palace, Placentia, and now hangs with a companion view of Whitehall in the Servants' Hall at Kingston Lacy in Dorset.

[37]

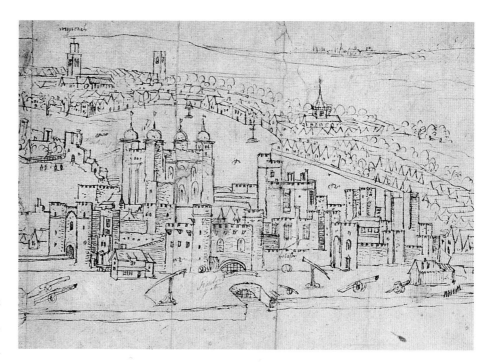

The Tower of London, from a sketch by Anthony van Wyngaerde, who visited England in the 1550s and drew the royal palaces along the Thames.

and finally, in the menagerie, 'having now for the eighth time also made a gratuity to the soldiers we returned to our hostel'.[45]

Once the major attractions in London – the Tower of London, Westminster Abbey and the Palace of Whitehall – were taken in, the foreign visitor left the capital for short excursions to Greenwich, Richmond Palace, Hampton Court, Windsor and the fabulous palace of Nonsuch, 'a place of such splendours that it overshadows the glory of all other buildings',[46] begun in 1538 by Henry VIII and completed during the reign of his daughter Mary. For those tourists who chose to venture further afield (and most did), the usual itinerary consisted of a circular tour to Oxford and Cambridge, with visits to those brand-new prodigy houses, Burghley, Theobalds and Holdenby, and, largely because of its place in recent history as the prison of Princess Elizabeth, Woodstock Palace in Oxfordshire.

One can see from this brief list that the buildings which formed the core of the Elizabethan 'Grand Tour' of England were a mixture of old and new, the old being the established royal palaces, and the new, those private houses built by private subjects. Unlike her father, Elizabeth herself built little of importance, preferring, as we have seen, to rely on and exploit her subjects' passion for architecture.

The reaction of the foreign tourist to these modern houses was generally favourable, although, as with most of the buildings which he visited, his enthusiasm was usually reserved for the contents rather than the architecture itself. Theobalds, according to the Duke of Pomerania-Wolgast, was 'one of the finest houses in England'; Jacob Rathgeb, visiting with his master the Duke of Würtemberg, noted that it was 'reckoned one of the most beautiful houses in England, which in truth it is'; and Waldstein thought that 'both the architecture and furnishings of this great house are magnificent', adding that 'it is notable for the number of its turrets and for its unrivalled fireplaces'.[47]

'Great', 'beautiful', 'the finest' – such epithets are the small change of sightseeing, and there is little evidence that the tourist was interested in detailed analysis of the form and disposition of elements within a building. Yet a critical vocabulary for the appreciation of buildings certainly did exist by this time: it reaches its most coherent expression in Sir Henry Wotton's *Elements of Architecture* (1624), where, in a 'methodical direction how to censure fabrics', Wotton elaborates on the four Vitruvian categories of *Eurythmia*, *Symmetria*, *Decor* and *Distributio*. Drawing on Palladio, Alberti and Renaissance theories of harmonic proportionality, Wotton describes *Eurythmia* as 'that agreeable harmony between the breadth, length and height of all the rooms of the fabric, which suddenly, where it is, taketh every beholder by the secret power of proportion'. *Symmetria* is more than symmetry, it is 'the convenience that runneth between the parts and the whole'. *Decor* is defined as a sort of architectural propriety, an absence of hubris: 'the keeping of a due respect between the inhabitant and the habitation'; and *Distributio* is the practical arrangement of elements within the building, 'that useful casting of all rooms for office, entertainment, or pleasure'.[48] In typical Renaissance fashion, Wotton and his contemporaries believed that by the systematic application of a set of criteria based around these four concepts, it was quite possible to arrive at an objective assessment of any architectural work.

So the techniques for evaluating and assessing any particular building *were* available to the late Elizabethans and Jacobeans. But we shouldn't be too surprised at the lack of a sophisticated Renaissance architectural vocabulary in the writings of this particular group of tourists. One would expect diarists like Waldstein and Platter and Rathgeb to be content with platitudes in describing the houses which they saw: they were, after all, sightseers rather than students of architecture, and the diaries in which they recorded their impressions were not intended as personal accounts of their own responses, but as records, impressionistic souvenirs of a foreign country, and perhaps as guidebooks for those who came after them. The travellers would often simply note down the words of their guide-interpreters; if they couldn't remember details of what they had seen, they would go to other sources. This is made abundantly clear when one compares accounts, and sees that whole passages, which were often written up from rough notes months, or even years, later, have been lifted either from Camden's *Britannia*, or even from those of their fellow-countrymen's diaries which had already been published in some form. Clare Williams, in her introduction to Thomas Platter's *Travels in England*, shows convincingly that Platter derived large sections of his travel writings from published sources: the whole of the first half of his chapter 'Of the Kingdom of England in general' is taken word for word from Sebastian Münster's *Cosmography*, while much of the second half is derived from Jacob Rathgeb's narrative of the

Duke of Würtemberg's 1592 itinerary, which was published in Tübingen in 1602.

In general, if there are few indications of a desire to understand the architecture of a house or palace, there is less evidence of an informed interest in its history. Like many of their English counterparts, this particular set of travellers accepted wildly inaccurate estimates of the age of particular buildings. Platter writes, without further comment: 'While we were drinking an evening draught in the village of Woodstock they told us that the palace was said to be erected in Julius Caesar's time.'[49] And almost every tourist remarks on the origins of the Tower of London, and in particular, its Norman keep: 'an old but strong castle built by Julius Caesar', according to Frederic Gerschow; 'a castle which is said to have been built by Julius Caesar', says Lupold von Wedel.[50] One wonders whether the attribution of early medieval and Romanesque work to the Romans was as common as it seems from contemporary sources. Evidence of a more discerning attitude comes from the musician Robert Laneham during a visit to Kenilworth in Warwickshire in 1575. He comments on the keep, 'that is called Caesar's Tower, rather ... for that it is square and high formed after the manner of Caesar's forts than that ever he built it'.[51]

But if the young German exploring England during the late sixteenth and early seventeenth centuries showed a certain naïvety over the nuances of architectural chronology, if he exhibited a lack of interest in the structural complexities of the royal palaces and prodigy houses which he saw, he more than made up for this by the sheer joy with which he responded to the contents of those palaces and houses, the paintings and tapestries, the unicorn's horns and birds of paradise, the cabinets of curiosities which were to form the centre-pieces of so many collections and attract so many new tourists during the next one hundred years.

CHAPTER 2

A Madness To Gaze At Trifles

Why do the rude vulgar so hastily post in a madness
To gaze at trifles, and toys not worthy the viewing?
And think them happy, when may be shew'd for a penny
The Fleet-street Mandrakes, that heavenly motion of Eltham,
Westminster monuments, and Guildhall huge Corinaeus,
That horn of Windsor (of a unicorn very likely,)
The cave of Merlin, the skirts of old Tom a Lincoln,
King John's sword at Linne, with the cup the Fraternity drink in,
The Tomb of Beauchamp, and sword of Guy a Warwick:
The great long Dutchman, and roaring Margaret a Barwick,
The Mummied Princes, and Caesar's wine yet in Dover,
Saint James his Guinea Hens, the Cassowary moreover . . .
Drake's ship at Deptford, King Richard's bed-stead i' Leicester,
The White Hall whale-bones, the silver Basin i' Chester;
The live-caught Dog-fish, the Wolf and Harry the Lion,
Hunks of the Bear-garden to be feared, if he be nigh on . . .

Henry Peacham, 1611[1]

THE TASTES OF TOURISTS have changed in any number of ways during the
last five hundred years: the things they have wanted to see, the things they have
been allowed to see and their responses to the experience, have all been conditioned by shifting social, architectural and artistic patterns of behaviour. But in
one respect their interests have remained constant. Ever since visits to a country
house or a royal palace ceased to be a merely social event, ever since tourists began
to be motivated by curiosity, they have been interested not so much in the architecture of a building as in what it contained, whether it be portraits or porcelain,
books or bedsteads.

One of the prerequisites of any interior has always been that it should be different: the items on show should be better, or stranger, or bigger, or costlier, than
those which form part of the visitor's own social and aesthetic milieu, and any
functional value which they may have had gave way, very early on, to their value as
display-objects.

In 1616, Justus Zinzerling could characterise Windsor simply by remarking that
'here is to be seen a unicorn's horn, nine spans long'. But just over eighty years
later, Celia Fiennes, who was certainly no connoisseur, praised the 'Hall which has

very fine paintings', and the 'Gallery full of pictures', although, ever practical, she did complain that some of the ceiling murals were 'so lofty it's enough to break one's neck to look on them'.[2]

However, Zinzerling's reference to unicorns doesn't mean that houses and palaces were devoid of more conventional attractions in the early 1600s. On the contrary, many were full of the most opulent and spectacular paintings and furnishings. During his 1602 visit to Theobalds, the Duke of Pomerania-Wolgast's secretary, Frederic Gerschow, remarked on the magnificent decorations, the splendid hangings, the velvet beds and chairs, the gilded panelling:

> Especially noteworthy were the three galleries. In the first were repres-entations of the principal emperors and knights of the Golden Fleece, with the most splendid cities in the world and their garments and fashions. In the next, the coats-of-arms of all the noble families of England, 20 in number, also all the viscounts and barons, about 42, the *labores Herculis*, and the game called billiards, on a long cloth-covered table. In the third, all England, represented by 52 trees, each tree representing one province. On the branches and leaves were pictured the coats-of-arms of all the dukes, earls, knights, and noblemen residing in the county; and between the trees, the towns and boroughs, together with the principal mountains and rivers.[3]

An integral part of the Elizabethan preoccupation with the conspicuous display of wealth centred on works of art. Sir Francis Walsingham kept an agent in Paris, who was charged with the job of finding and buying pictures. The Long Gallery at Hardwick in 1601 contained thirty-nine paintings, including portraits of Bess, Queen Elizabeth and the Virgin Mary.[4] And Whitehall, like most of the royal palaces, contained large quantities of portraits and 'histories', including:

> the meeting of the Emperor Maximilian I and Henry VIII near Tournai and Therouanne; King Henry VIII's entry into – and his magnificent display at – Boulogne; . . . the battle of Maximilian I and Pope Julius II with Louis XII of France before Ravenna on Easter Day 1512, where 23 thousand men lost their lives; and a genealogical table of the Kings of England.[5]

By their very nature, murals, portraits, statuary and fine furnishings were the prerogative of the wealthy. They were not, however, brought together according to a specific aesthetic programme. When one looks at the structure of aristocratic collections at the end of Elizabeth's reign, it is possible to discern two clear motives in their composition: on the one hand, paintings were designed to inspire or to convey to the visitor the status of the owner's connections and relationships with important figures of the day; on the other hand, objects were collected for their rarity, their craftsmanship, or often simply for their sheer curiosity value.

This first point – that paintings, which were almost invariably portraits, were bought and shown for their subject-matter rather than for the excellence of their

execution – is neatly illustrated in Lord Herbert of Cherbury's account of a visit to Dorset House in the Strand, London. He was unacquainted with the Earl of Dorset, but the latter invited him into his gallery, 'and showing me many pictures, he at last brought me to a frame covered with green taffeta, and asked me who I thought was there; and therewithal presently drawing the curtain, showed me my own picture'.[6] Dorset knew, of course, of Herbert's reputation as a soldier, statesman, poet and philosopher, and, desiring a picture of such a notable figure, he had managed to obtain a copy of his portrait. He regarded it, not as an art-object to be judged according to a set of aesthetic criteria, but as the equivalent of a photograph, a likeness of a famous contemporary. In a similar fashion, Lord Howard of Bindon asked Lord Salisbury for his portrait, which he wished to hang 'in the

A watercolour by David Cox of the Long Gallery at Hardwick Hall, painted in the nineteenth century after the restoration work undertaken by the 6th Duke of Devonshire. Evoking the spirit of his ancestress, Bess of Hardwick, the Duke covered the tapestries with as many family portraits as he could find.

Bess of Hardwick, a portrait painted in the 1590s in her last widowhood when she was building the New Hall. This portrait may originally have been in her Withdrawing Chamber, but now hangs alongside pictures of her husbands, family, and the kings and queens of England and Scotland in the Long Gallery at Hardwick.

gallery I lately made for the pictures of sundry of my honourable friends, whose presentation thereby to behold will greatly delight me to walk often in that place where I may see so comfortable a sight'.[7]

In other words, portraits were valued by their owners for their associations rather than for their execution, and the visitor's response was conditioned by historical and political, rather than aesthetic, considerations. The 1613 journal of the Duke of Saxe-Weimar's visit to England shows the royal palaces containing a pretty representative cross-section of European royalty and nobility, ranging from past and present kings and queens of England, through 'the present Elector of Brandenburg, in complete armour, with regimental baton' and Don John of Austria, to Bathory, King of Poland, 'all the Turkish Emperors', and 'Gaspar Coligny, Admiral of France, who perished with his brothers in the massacre at Paris'.[8] Nowhere is any mention made of the artists who painted these pictures, and no doubt the Duke, insofar as he brought any critical apparatus to bear on the paintings at Whitehall, or Nonsuch or Windsor, would have agreed with the sentiments expressed in Richard Haydocke's 1598 *Tracte Containing the Artes of curious Paintinge Carving & Buildinge*, itself a translation from a work by the Milanese artist Giovanni Paolo Lomazzo: 'Painting is an art; because it imitateth natural things most precisely, and is the counterfeiter and (as it were) the very ape of nature: whose quantity, eminence, and colours, it ever striveth to imitate.'[9]

For most seventeenth-century tourists, the success of a portrait depended on the extent to which it successfully represented reality rather than upon any intrinsic merit; they assumed, almost without question, that painting was 'only the imitation of the surface of Nature'.[10] If they happened to know the sitter, then critical comparison was possible. More often, they viewed a portrait as an announcement of the status of its owner, and, of course, as an opportunity to display their own knowledge of contemporary events or of social and political history. John Evelyn, himself one of the great connoisseurs of his day, epitomises this attitude in 1689, in his complaint at the way in which artists omitted the names of their subjects from portraits:

> I am in perfect indignation at this folly, as oft as I consider what extravagant sums are given for a dry scalp of some (forsooth) Italian painting, be it of Raphael or Titian himself; which would be infinitely more estimable were we assured it was the picture of the learned Count of Mirandola, Politian, Guicciardini, Machiavel, Petrarch, Ariosto, or Tasso; or some famous pope, prince, poet, or other hero of those times.[11]

The value of a portrait resided in its subject; and the visitor walking in the Long Gallery at Hardwick Hall would be expected to admire the person rather than the painting, whether he was looking at 'the picture of our Lady the Virgin Mary', 'Queen Elizabeth's picture in a less table', or Rowland Lockey's portrait of Bess of Hardwick herself.[12]

A tortoise from Lady Wilson's cabinet of curiosities at Wallington in Northumberland. Although her cabinet dates from the eighteenth century, the contents resemble those of the seventeenth century in their eclecticism.

However, paintings were very far from being the only contents of a house to call forth comment during the later sixteenth and seventeenth centuries. Hangings and sculptures – the sorts of thing that we would regard as conventional art-objects today – were on show at all of the royal palaces. Platter commented on the fine tapestries and the stone statues of three Roman emperors at Nonsuch, and Lupold von Wedel was particularly impressed by the 'fine chimney-piece with the royal arms cut in a stone as clear as crystal, with two lions as supporters', which he saw in the Privy Council chamber at Whitehall.[13] Like pictures, such things were the preserve of the wealthy, serving to demonstrate the owner's status.

Tourists' responses were not primarily aesthetic: they wanted to see all that was rare and costly, and, during the first part of the century at least, there was no sense of their responding differently to a painting, a tapestry, a piece of clockwork or a curiosity of nature. They were ready to be impressed and amazed by anything that was outside their normal sphere of experience. We have already seen that visitors

to the royal apartments at Windsor remarked on the unicorn's horn (originally the property of a narwhal); they were just as impressed by the stuffed bird of paradise in the Queen's bed-chamber. At Richmond, there was a mirror 'in which Henry VII was able to see what he wished; but this mirror broke in pieces of itself when the King died'. Richmond also contained the room in which Henry VII died, 'the wall of which is besprinkled with his blood, but this is not permitted to be seen by everyone'. The Palace of Whitehall also offered a mirror, 'which shows many faces when one looks into it',[14] together with a clockwork celestial globe and an immense whale rib; and at Hampton Court there was a horn cup which was said to break into pieces if poison were put into it. (One wonders how they could have known.)

The most intriguing collection of curiosities to be part of the tourist route at the turn of the century did not, however, belong to the royal family: it was to be seen at Sir Walter Cope's house in London. In addition to some fine paintings and a

John Eveleyn's cabinet, now in the Geffrye Museum in London. Made in Paris in 1652, it is of ebony decorated with engraved scenes and flowers. He would have used it to keep his papers and valuables safe in his closet, sometimes confusingly known as a cabinet.

RITRATTO DEL MVSEO DI
FERRANTE, IMPERATO

Ferrante Imperato's famous cabinet of natural history curiosities in Naples, as shown on the title page of *Dell'Historia naturale* published in 1599. This book was part of Sir Richard Ellys' collection now at Blickling (p.55).

Hieronymus Janssens' *A Picture Gallery with Fashionable Visitors*, painted in the 1660s and now hanging at Uppark in Sussex. Although it is probably an allegory, contrasting the precious objects on the left-hand table against *The Last Judgement* in the foreground, it also provides a good record of a gentleman's collection of the period.

delightful garden, Cope – a Fellow of the Society of Antiquaries who had travelled extensively – was able to show 'an apartment, stuffed with queer foreign objects in every corner'.[15] This astonishing array of oddities (the first well-documented collection in England) included two teeth of a sea-horse, a rhinoceros horn, an embalmed child, a Chinese cap made out of goosefeet, an Indian chain made out of monkey's teeth, fire flies, an Indian canoe, a round horn which 'had grown out of an English woman's forehead', clothes from China, Arabia and Java, saddles, musical instruments and weapons, and a remora, 'a little fish which holds up or hinders boats from sailing when it touches them, likewise another species called "torpedo" which petrifies and numbs the crews' hands if it so much as touches the oars'.[16] Cope's cabinet of curiosities was not the only museum in London – a number of antiquaries were bringing together catholic collections of coins, medals, fossils, manuscripts and weird artefacts of all kinds, and Platter records that 'in one house on the Thames bridge I beheld a large live camel'.[17] But it was reckoned to be the best and the strangest, or rather, the best because it was the strangest.

The cabinet of curiosities, or closet of rarities, which was to become such a significant item on the tourist's agenda during the seventeenth century, has its roots in the *Kunstkammern*, *Wunderkammern* and *studioli* which had grown to be an important part of aristocratic life on the Continent during the sixteenth century. These collections of works of art, archaeological and botanical specimens, exotica and quirks of nature varied enormously in scope, arrangement and in the motivating forces behind them. The grandest, the encyclopaedic and intensely personal *studioli* of Italian princes like Francesco I de' Medici, were assembled, not for scientific or scholarly research purposes, but as attempts to recreate the world in microcosm, symbols of the owner's immense power and dominion over all things natural and artificial. To begin with, these collections were private, and open to very few outside a prince's own circle: but by the end of the sixteenth century their more public role in enhancing their owner's reputation and confirming his status was recognised, as can be seen by Francesco I's decision in 1580 to convert the top floor of the grand-ducal public offices at the Uffizi into a show-place for his art collections and scientific curiosities.

At the same time, research collections were also growing up on the Continent, dedicated to function and scholarship. One of the most famous was that of the Veronese pharmacist Francesco Calceolari, whose museum was open to his pupils, and who issued a printed catalogue in 1584. In Bologna, the professor of natural philosophy and director of the botanical gardens at the University, Ulisse Aldrovandi, amassed an enormous cabinet, which by 1595 contained around 11,000 fruits, animals and minerals, 8,000 tempera illustrations and 7,000 dried plants. Their function, unlike the private or public displays of Aldrovandi's social superiors, was not only to provoke wonder, delight and pride in ownership, but also to afford opportunities for study and research.

Right: Portrait of
Thomas Howard, 2nd
Earl of Arundel by
Daniel Mytens, painted
*c.*1618. As one of
England's great
seventeenth-century art
collectors, he is depicted
with his statue gallery at
his London home,
Arundel House, in
the background. A
companion portrait
shows his Countess,
Aletheia, seated in front
of their picture gallery
(*far right*).

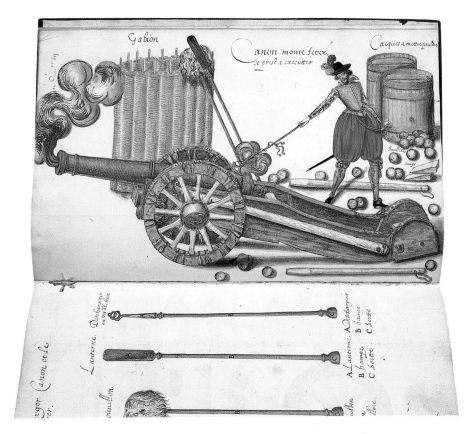

Some English collections had a heavy bias towards the arts, others towards science; many consisted of a mixture, and one needs to bear in mind that in the early seventeenth century the distinction between the two was blurred. But most were heavily influenced by continental practice, as the example of the greatest of early collectors, Thomas Howard, Earl of Arundel, Horace Walpole's 'father of vertu in England', demonstrates.

Encouraged by his father-in-law, the seventh Earl of Shrewsbury, to take an interest in the arts, Arundel travelled widely in Europe. In Antwerp in 1612 he recorded that his guide 'hath let me want the sight of no curiosity',[18] and over the next few years he spent time in Italy, not only viewing the cabinets and galleries of dukes and princes, but also acquiring the basis of what was perhaps the first great English art collection. By the 1630s, largely through the labours of a network of agents on the Continent, Arundel had amassed a magnificent cabinet of drawings and prints, classical antiquities, books and manuscripts, and precious and semi-precious stones. As well as individual items, he purchased other entire collections, including, in 1636, the Pirckheimer Library, which contained sketches, notebooks and diaries of Dürer, and, also in the 1630s, the famous gem cabinet of Daniel Nys, which, according to John Evelyn, cost the Earl £10,000.

Arundel belonged to the set which gathered around Henry, Prince of Wales, in the years before the Prince's death in 1612. He was also instrumental in teaching Henry's younger brother, later Charles I – himself a considerable patron of the arts – the value of art as a means of enhancing the dignity and prestige of a great man; a lesson which Arundel himself had learned through his experiences in Italy.

The importance of continental practice for the well-born Englishman engaged in assembling a cabinet of art-objects and curiosities was widely acknowledged in the 1600s. Virtuosi, as such collectors became known, even took their title from their Italian counterparts. Henry Peacham, a tutor at Arundel House, was the first known to use the term, discussing classical antiquities in 1634: 'The possession of such rarities, by reason of their deadly costliness, doth properly belong to princes, or rather to princely minds … Such as are skilled in them, are by the *Italians* termed *Virtuosi.*'[19]

An important element in the rise of the virtuoso was learning for its own sake rather than as a means of improving the human condition. This attitude was slowly becoming part of the cultural apparatus of the ruling class, in a way that was unheard of in the sixteenth century. Bess of Hardwick was by no means unlettered, but in 1601 'my lady's books' (kept in her bedchamber at Hardwick Hall) numbered just six. Bess was a woman of action, not a scholar: her accomplishments were only of value in so far as they were means to an end, and learning for learning's sake would have seemed pointless to her, as it would to most Elizabethans. Even when a courtier was encouraged to pursue scholarly or cultural studies, the end was social ornament as an integral part of a well-rounded character; such studies were still not seen as occupations of any intrinsic merit.

But this attitude was to change during the seventeenth century. When, in *The Advancement of Learning* (1605), Bacon criticised men who have 'entered into a desire of learning and knowledge, sometimes upon a natural curiosity and inquisitive appetite; sometimes to entertain their minds with variety and delight; sometimes for ornament and reputation … as if there were sought in knowledge … a tower of state, for a proud mind to raise itself upon',[20] he was highlighting what were to become two of the most important features of the virtuoso collector: a pursuit of rarities and curiosities for their own sake; and an awareness that such collections were methods of enhancing and defining status.

Beginning as instruments for discovering who was the right sort and who wasn't, study and the acquisition of cultural and scientific artefacts became in themselves a way of marking out the quality from the *hoi polloi*; Peacham advocated the study of heraldry as a way of enabling one to 'discern and know an intruding upstart, shot up with the last night's mushroom, from an ancient descended and deserved gentleman'.[21] By the 1670s, the virtuoso Obadiah Walker was recommending that part of a young gentleman's education should consist of 'ingenious studies … such as poorer persons are not able to support'.[22] The implication is clear: the fact that 'poorer persons' were not able to pursue such studies

The plaster ceiling of the Long Gallery at Blickling is decorated with central panels containing heraldic achievements, symbols of the Five Senses and of Learning. The latter image and a series of twenty emblems running down either side were chosen from Henry Peacham's *Minerva Britanna*, published in 1612. This detail shows *Pulchritudo Fominea.*

PVLCHRITVDO FŒMINEA

(and here Walker was referring to antiquities, natural history and astronomy) was one of the things that distinguished the virtuoso as a member of a privileged elite. And it was not simply his learned conversation that displayed that distinction: his collection became a physical expression of his learning and hence his social standing. While many virtuosi were genuinely interested in the pursuit of learning for 'benefit and use', in Bacon's words, and the Royal Society, founded in the year of the Restoration, had its roots in the virtuoso movement, one motive at least for the assembling of a collection does seem to have been an awareness of the status which could be achieved by its owner.

A country-house closet, which in the sixteenth century might have housed a maid, a few trunks of clothes and a close-stool, could, by the later seventeenth century, have become a private and mysterious place, open to none but its owner and a few initiates, where precious gems, coins and paintings were carefully stored and gloated over. The Green Closet at Ham House in Surrey may well have been such an inner sanctum: only four metres by five, it was lavishly decorated and filled with portraits and miniatures, a special, secret place where, in the 1670s, the Duke and Duchess of Lauderdale could keep their most treasured possessions.

At the other end of the spectrum was the famous, and virtually unprecedentedly accessible, Tradescant collection, housed in what was known as 'The Ark' at Lambeth. John Tradescant the elder, who died in 1638, travelled widely, both in the Low Countries and France, and further afield, to Russia and the Barbary Coast. He was thus able to view foreign cabinets and also to acquire specimens for his own, while, through the good offices of his patron, the Duke of Buckingham, he could enlist the help of merchants travelling in the Americas and the Near East, asking that they bring back 'all manner of beasts and fowls and birds alive or if not with heads, horns, beaks, claws, skins, feathers; slips or seeds, plants, trees or shrubs . . . and also from the East Indies with shells, stones, bones, egg-shells with what cannot come alive'.[23] The result was a collection that by 1634 took a full day to tour, and one that was open to ordinary visitors – on payment of a sixpenny admission fee. It was augmented by Tradescant's son, and on the death of Tradescant the younger's widow, was bequeathed to the virtuoso and antiquary Elias Ashmole, thus forming the core of the Ashmolean Museum when it was founded in Oxford in the 1680s.

Besides the botanical and biological specimens, the Tradescant collection contained large numbers of 'artificial' items: cameos and intaglios, weapons, coins and medals. When John Evelyn visited Lambeth in 1657, he noted in his diary: 'The chiefest rarities were, in my opinion, the ancient Roman, Indian and other nations' armour, shields, and weapons; some habits of curiously-coloured and wrought feathers, one from the phoenix wing as tradition goes.'[24] It was certainly of considerable historical and scientific importance, in spite of the inclusion of items like the phoenix feather. But it was also a major tourist attraction, and no doubt the many visitors who turned up to see it were motivated less by a desire to

The Green Closet at Ham, designed to display cabinet pictures and miniatures. In 1677 fifty-seven pictures belonging to the Duke and Duchess of Lauderdale were recorded as hanging here, in frames of gilt and ebony.

further their pursuit of learning than by a wish to see, in Tradescant the elder's words, 'the biggest that can be gotten . . . any thing that is strange'.[25]

By the later years of the century, the virtuoso, with his wide-ranging interests and his cabinet of curiosities, had become a figure of fun, a stock character in the satirist's repertoire. Thomas Shadwell's 1676 play, *The Virtuoso*, gave London audiences Sir Nicholas Gimcrack, a pseudo-scientist who has taken the pursuit of knowledge for its own sake to absurd lengths. Learning to swim by lying on a table and imitating the motions of a frog, he declares that he has no intention of putting his skill into practice in the water: 'I content myself with the speculative part of swimming. I care not for the practick. I seldom bring any thing to use; 'tis not my way. Knowledge is my ultimate end.'[26] Gimcrack is almost exclusively interested in scientific research, as opposed to aesthetics and the study of antiquities, and most of Shadwell's satire is directed against the varied researches of Robert Boyle, John Evelyn and their fellow-experimenters in the Royal Society, the spiritual heirs of Walter Cope rather than of the Earl of Arundel. The truth was that virtuosi and their cabinets of curiosities were going out of fashion in the face of such public ridicule; their catholic tastes were being replaced by a more clearly defined aesthetic sensibility.

By the early years of the eighteenth century, the country house was fast becoming a repository for works of art rather than curiosities. When the two young sons of William Blathwayt, of Dyrham Park in Gloucestershire, spent three hours touring Burghley in May 1703, their tutor recorded: '[N]othing is comparable to the large number of costly Italian paintings which form the chief decoration; one sees there among other things in one room a marble statue that we were assured had cost seventeen hundred crowns in Rome.'[27] Twenty years later Daniel Defoe also remarked on the pictures at Burghley, praising them and pointing out that they had been amassed as a result of foreign travel. The Earl of Exeter visited Italy three times, and the Duke of Tuscany himself assisted the Earl 'to purchase many excellent pieces at reasonable prices'. The result was a superb collection: 'It would be endless to give a detail of the fine pieces his lordship brought from Italy, all originals, and by the best masters; 'tis enough to say, they infinitely exceed all that can be seen in England, and are of more value than the house itself, and all the park belonging to it.'[28]

The Grand Tour of Europe was rapidly gaining in popularity among the landed classes, and during the eighteenth century a country house's galleries would come to contain not only portraits of friends and relatives, but also antique marbles and old masters; its cabinet would house not weird and wonderful specimens of natural history, or mechanical contrivances, but miniatures and intaglios. The age of the virtuoso, with his naïve delight in the bizarre or exotic, was ending, but his legacy to the Georgian tourist was a country house which could boast collections worth viewing, and a cultural climate in which the desire to see those collections had become a legitimate activity among persons of taste.

CHAPTER 3

Arbiters of Taste

Some ne'er advance a judgment of their own,
But catch the spreading notion of the town . . .
Alexander Pope, *Essay on Criticism*, 1729[1]

CELIA FIENNES, the Nonconformist granddaughter of William, Viscount Saye and Sele, has become the most famous of early tourists, largely as a result of the publication of her *Journeys*, in an abridged form in 1888, and complete in 1947. Celia travelled the length and breadth of England in a series of excursions in the late 1680s and 1690s, 'to regain my health by variety and change of air and exercise'.[2] While she was interested in everything she saw, from natural scenery to local industry to architecture, it was the new that really fired her imagination: the late medieval Haddon Hall in Derbyshire, for example, was 'a good old house . . . but nothing very curious'; and Lichfield Cathedral in Staffordshire was 'a stately structure but old'.[3]

Modern buildings, on the other hand, attracted both detailed comment and the greatest praise. Uppark in Sussex, built between 1685 and 1690 for the first Earl of Tankerville, was 'very neat . . . in the midst of fine gardens, gravel and grass walks'.[4] At Chatsworth in Derbyshire, which Talman was rebuilding for the first Duke of Devonshire, Celia admired the Laguerre murals, the elaborate waterworks, and the 'curious carving'.[5]

When Celia visited the Earl of Chesterfield's Bretby in Derbyshire in the course of her 'great journey to Newcastle and to Cornwall' in 1698, she found the Jacobean mansion pleasant, but rather old-fashioned: 'The roof is not flat as our modern buildings so the garret windows come out on the tiling which is all of slate; none of the windows are sashes which in my opinion is the only thing it wants to render it a complete building.'[6] After examining the outside of the house, Celia went on to view the various interiors. She was unable to get into the drawing-room, 'the Earl having just married his eldest daughter Lady Mary to one Mr Cooke, a gentleman of a good estate hard by [Thomas Coke, of nearby Melbourne Hall]', but she did not allow the celebrations to detract from her visit: she was still able to see the marble hall, chapel, parlour and 'a large room with a billiard table', besides admiring the crimson velvet bed in the bridal chamber itself.

But 'that which is most admired – and justly so to be – by all persons and excite their curiosity to come and see' were the gardens, which were scarcely thirty years old, and the waterworks, which were still being laid out by the Frenchman Grillet.

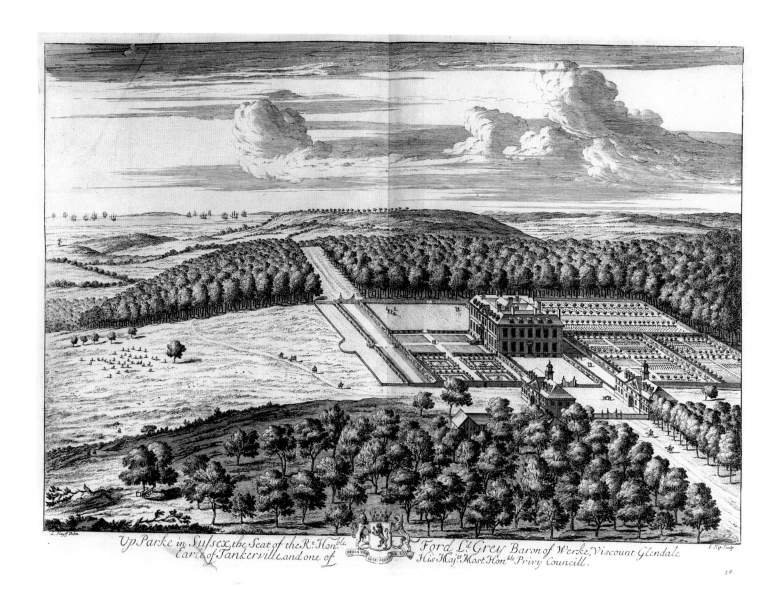

Up Parke in Suſsex, the Seat of the Rt Honble Earle of Tankerville, and one of
Ford Ld Grey Baron of Werke, Viscount Glendale His Majsty Most Honble Privy Councill.

L. Knyff Delin.

I. Kip Sculp.

38

Lord Tankerville's house and formal gardens at Uppark, as drawn by Leonard Knyff and engraved by Johannes Kip for *Britannia Illustrata*, 1707. When Celia Fiennes visited Uppark, she commended the fine gardens, gravel and grass walks.

These were much more to Celia's taste than the house itself: the formality of the gravel walks and canals, the avenues of orange and lemon trees 'in boxes', and the rows of potted flowers and shrubs all appealed to her essentially Baroque imagination, while the fountains and water-jets delighted her. Having seen all there was to see, she was shown into a 'cool room in which was a fountain, where I drank a glass of wine'.[7] That she was offered this hospitality at a time when the family was not only in residence but celebrating a marriage is significant, for it confirms the maintenance, in some form, of the medieval tradition of good housekeeping. Celia was certainly not the only tourist exploring Britain in the 1690s (her brief reference to the gardens at Bretby as a famous sight admired by all indicates a growth in tourism), but it seems clear that, as yet, numbers had not grown sufficiently to undermine the long-standing conventions regulating the conduct of owner and visitor, a relationship that was still essentially one of host and guest.

Informal codes and social structures were developing to accommodate the occasions where a total stranger arrived on the doorstep and asked to wander round your house, but they grew out of the existing conventions. Senior members of the domestic staff, whose job it had been to vet and grade visitors asking for hospitality, began to do the same with tourists, and often showed them over the house, expecting a financial reward in return. Sixty years after Celia Fiennes' journeys of discovery, when the medieval conventions of good lordship and hospitality had all but withered away, even such a well-known connoisseur as Horace Walpole would not set out on an excursion without taking the precaution of writing beforehand, 'for leave to see every thing, in case [a family] should not be at home, or had given general orders for not showing their houses'.[8] And by this time the country-house visitor had become a commonplace, a figure of fun:

> In the vacant season of the year
> Some Templar gay begins his wild career;
> From seat to seat o'er pompous scenes he flies,
> Views all with equal wonder and surprise,
> Till, sick of domes, arcades, and temples, grown,
> He hies fatigued, not satisfied, to Town.[9]

There are three major reasons for this change in attitude: there were more houses to visit; there was more to see, both inside and out; and, most important of all, the prevailing cultural climate made an acquaintance with art and architecture an integral part of upper-class social behaviour.

The mania for architecture which began after the accession of William III and which rapidly gained ground during the early years of the eighteenth century caused some comment at the time. 'All the world are running mad after building, as far as they can reach', noted John Vanbrugh in 1708;[10] while less than twenty years later, Daniel Defoe, in the preface to the first edition of his *Tour Through England and Wales*, remarked that 'Even while the sheets are in the press, new beauties appear in several places, and almost to every part we are oblig'd to add appendixes, and supplemental accounts of fine houses, new undertakings, buildings, &c.'[11]

This building boom had its roots in the displays of wealth and prestige constructed by the newly powerful and newly secure Whig ruling class in the wake of the Glorious Revolution. Just as William III himself had Wren remodel Hampton Court, so the Whig aristocracy, anxious to make their mark, rebuilt on their own estates during the 1690s and early 1700s: the Duke of Devonshire at Chatsworth, the Earl of Carlisle at Castle Howard in Yorkshire, and so on down the social scale, through King William's Secretary of State for War, William

Above: James Thornhill's delightful drawing of Hanbury Hall in Worcestershire, *c*.1710. Hanbury was built in the opening years of the eighteenth century by Thomas Vernon, a successful barrister: he chose the comfortable style of Restoration architecture, with a central cupola and dormer windows in a hipped roof. But he made some dramatic additions, including a painted staircase in the grand baroque style, which he commissioned from James Thornhill.

Right: Thomas Vernon's monument by Edward Stanton and Christopher Horsnaile in Hanbury Church.

Blathwayt, who rebuilt Dyrham Park, to Thomas Vernon, the Whig lawyer and MP who commissioned a new house at Hanbury in Worcestershire at the beginning of the eighteenth century. After the hiatus caused by the political and military disruptions of the middle years of the century and the uneasy and uncertain peace of the Restoration, building as a demonstration of status had become as fashionable as it had been one hundred years earlier.

As a result of the activities of the virtuosi and their cabinets of curiosities, the country houses that were springing up all over the country held contents that were very different from those of the late sixteenth and early seventeenth centuries. Perhaps the most significant difference was the preponderance of continental paintings and sculpture on display. The notes which Horace Walpole made during his various tours between July 1751 and 1780 bear witness to the change of emphasis from portraits of family and friends to art-objects collected as such, and brought from Italy, France and the Low Countries. At Uppark in Sussex, for instance, there were pictures of the owner and his wife, to be sure – but they were done by

[64]

Pompeo Batoni, the leading Italian portrait painter of his day; there were also 'four wax basreliefs coloured, and done at Naples of Massaniello and his associates'.[12] Knole, in Kent, could boast 'an antique statue of Pythagoras, bought by the present Duke. The head is good, but the statue is not of the first workmanship. His Grace has bought a few good pictures, particularly a satyr and woman by Annibale Carracci.'[13] And at Stourhead in Wiltshire – 'the rooms of the house are in general too low, but are richly furnished' – there was a magnificent array of Carlo Dolcis, Sebastian Riccis, Poussins and Canalettos. Singled out for special mention was:

> The Marquis Palavicini crowned with laurels by Glory, and directed by his genius to the temple of virtue, Pallas instructing Fame to inscribe his character in letters of gold on her shield; Carlo Maratta accompanied and inspired by the Graces drawing his portrait. This picture, of which the figures are large as life, was painted by Carlo, and purchased from the Arnaldi collection at Florence, which contained the remains of the Palavicini collection (of which many pieces are at Houghton).[14]

Englishmen were taking an active interest in the flourishing European art market. Henry Hoare obtained many of the works of art at Stourhead while touring in Italy in the 1720s and 1730s, and, like those of so many of his contemporaries, the wealthy banker's collection was the result of purchases – some shrewd and discriminating, many less so – made during a Grand Tour. Just as their German counterparts had visited England in the last years of Elizabeth's reign as a means of furthering their education, so, by the early 1700s, scores of young Englishmen, with tutors (known as 'bear-leaders') in tow, followed in the footsteps of Lord Arundel, and, more significantly, John Evelyn, Roger Pratt and other gentlemen and aristocrats who had turned their backs on Civil War and Commonwealth and travelled on the Continent during the 1640s. Some reacted with a xenophobic chauvinism to all things foreign. Others embraced European society wholeheartedly, and occasionally quite literally, as James Boswell was to do later in the century, celebrating Ash Wednesday 1765 in Rome with a vow to have a different woman every day. But for most, a primary function of their Tour was the sight of both classical antiquities and the great Renaissance collections.

Some of these Grand Tourists could hardly be described as connoisseurs. They were young men in their late teens or early twenties, intent on having a good time. If they had to 'do' Venice or Rome, then it was in as perfunctory a manner as possible, like the unnamed gentleman described by John Moore, who spent almost the whole of his six-week stay in Rome engaged in more congenial pursuits, but who, when the time came for him to leave, felt unable to return home without being able to say that he had seen the sights:

> He ordered a post-chaise and four horses to be ready early in the morning,
> and driving through churches, palaces, villas, and ruins, with all possible

Marchese Pallavicini and the Artist, painted by Carlo Maratta in 1705. The picture, celebrating Pallavicini's achievements as a patron of the arts, was bought for Henry Hoare in 1758 by Horace Mann, the British Representative in Florence. Hung by Hoare at Stourhead, it excited particular note from eighteenth-century visitors.

The Cognoscenti by the eighteenth-century artist, Thomas Patch, now in the North Gallery at Petworth. Patch, whose self-portrait hangs on the wall, pokes fun at the pretensions of the English as connoisseurs on the Grand Tour.

expedition, he fairly saw, in two days, all that we had beheld during our crawling course of six weeks. I found afterwards that we had not the advantage of him in a single picture, or the most mutilated remnant of a statue.[15]

Others, however, took their Tour much more seriously, regarding it as an opportunity to learn languages, to take classes in dancing and music, and to exercise and develop their taste in art. Typical of this more earnest breed was Henry Lee Warner of Walsingham Abbey in Norfolk, who was abroad between 1713 and 1716. Writing to his uncle from Leghorn in October 1714, he announced that 'we can already see the difference between the Italian and French painting and architecture'; and armed with a letter of introduction from a neighbour, Sir Henry

Dr James Hay, a Bear-leader, by Leone Ghezzi. In a letter to Horace Mann in 1749, Horace Walpole refers to travelling governors as bear-leaders, talking of 'forty dozen bears and bear-leaders that you have been endeavouring for those thirty years to tame, and the latter half of which never are licked into form'.

Right: Sir Matthew Fetherstonhaugh inherited a huge fortune from a distant relative, and used part of the money to buy himself a country house, Uppark, in 1747. Two years later he embarked with his wife, Sarah (*far right*), on the Grand Tour to the principal Italian cities. The young couple had their portraits painted by the fashionable Pompeo Batoni during their visit to Rome in 1751.

Bedingfield of Oxburgh Hall, he presented himself at the Court in Florence, where the Grand Duke gave 'particular orders for to see his medals and his armoury which are esteemed as great favours. He has the greatest collection of the best pictures and medals I ever saw.'[16]

Still in Italy, Warner also remarked to his uncle: 'I could not avoid buying some pictures and prints which are the chief manufactures of that country'; it was the developing international art market that was to be of most importance to the English country house. To have one's portrait painted by Rosalba Carriera or Pompeo Batoni, 'the best modern painter, very fat',[17] was only one side of the business: professional dealers like de Bary in Amsterdam and Cardinal Allesandro Albani (also a famous collector) in Rome catered for the English tourist's desire for art-objects, both as souvenirs and as the core of a collection befitting a man of taste. Henry Hoare at Stourhead, the Earl of Exeter at Burghley, Thomas Coke at Holkham and William Windham at Felbrigg were just a few of the patrons who drew together works of art while on the Grand Tour.

Nor did these collections cease to grow when the travellers returned home. Their tastes formed and moulded during their tour, country-house owners continued to maintain an interest in various pieces coming onto the market in France, Holland and Italy. Robert Walpole, who never in fact toured abroad, made good use of his relatives as agents during their travels, as a means of importing paintings and sculptures for his new house at Houghton in Norfolk. His brother Horatio, for example, was a diplomat in Paris in the 1720s; writing to Robert in 1726, he said: 'As to the pictures, the Raphael was sold two days before I received your letter; for 1900 livres which is now about £950 ster[ling]. There remains still the Guido, the Paul Veronese and there is an old Palma that is an excellent picture.'[18] Four years later, Robert Walpole's son Edward was acting as his agent in Rome: 'I have seen every statue and piece of that kind of antiquity that is worth seeing in Rome among which there is nothing to be had that could possibly serve your purpose. Those that are valuable and most entire are either entail'd or in the hands of people that won't part with them.'[19]

Such was the volume of trade being carried out in Europe, and in Italy in particular, that by the early eighteenth century the Papal States had established a mechanism for controlling the export of major works of art. Thomas Coke was arrested and threatened with imprisonment for attempting to export a headless statue of Diana without a licence, while the young architect Matthew Brettingham, who worked as Coke's agent in Rome for eight years in the late 1740s and early 1750s, was involved in complicated negotiations and a lawsuit before he could ship one particular batch of antique sculptures back to Holkham. Statues of Ceres and Minerva, both bought from Cardinal Albani, and of Meleager, Cybele and Venus, were all granted licences on the grounds that they had been heavily restored; but these licences were suddenly revoked by Cardinal Valenti, Secretary of State to Pope Benedict XIV. The statues were examined by experts, and it was agreed that all but the Cybele would be allowed to leave the country. The system of export

The Fetherstonhaughs' Grand Tour lasted for two years, during which they bought many furnishings to enrich Uppark. One such purchase was a pair of scagliola tops for tables, commissioned from Don Petro Belloni in Florence. Don Petro was assistant to the Abbot of the monastery of Vallombrosa, who was principally responsible for developing scagliola, plaster made from pulverised gypsum, into a fine art form. The Uppark table tops, decorated with landscapes and flowers, are a particularly magnificent example, taking over five years to make.

permissions seems to have related only to antiquities, but the mere fact that it was operating at all shows both a sophisticated awareness of a cultural heritage in Italy – the product of the Renaissance – and the impact on that heritage of commercial trafficking in art-objects – also a product of the Renaissance, and a legacy of the acquisitive Italian princes of the sixteenth and seventeenth centuries.

It was not only paintings and statuary that appealed to the enthusiastic tourist. As Celia Fiennes's experiences at Bretby demonstrate, gardens were also a major attraction. Bretby was famous throughout the country for Grillet's waterworks. So was another of Grillet's creations, Chatsworth, where, in 1697, Celia marvelled over the 'fine gardens one without another with gravel walks and squares of grass with stone statues in them and in the middle of each garden is a large fountain full of images sea gods and dolphins and sea horses which are full of pipes which spout out water in the bason and spouts all about the gardens'.[20] Scarcely pausing to draw breath, she singled out for special praise an artificial willow: 'The leaves bark and all looks very natural, the root is full of rubbish or great stones to appearance, and all on a sudden by turning a sluice it rains from each leaf and from the branches like a shower, it being made of brass and pipes to each leaf but in appearance is exactly like any willow.'[21]

The fountain obviously did not look 'exactly like any willow' to a visitor to Chatsworth a century later, who dismissed the curiosity in a few words: 'There is also a tin tree, which, as you approach it, the leaves spit out water.'[22] However, at the time such elaborate displays fascinated friends, guests and tourists alike, and achieved some renown during a period when water-power was first being harnessed both inside and outside the country house. But it was the even more elaborate, if less overtly artificial, garden landscapes of the first half of the eighteenth century which attracted most visitors: the temples, grottos and carefully designed vistas of gardens like Hagley and the Leasowes, both in Herefordshire, Stowe in Buckinghamshire and Stourhead in Wiltshire were intended to be seen by outsiders from the first, and many achieved enormous celebrity, with guidebooks and plans, opening times and, by the end of the century, tea-rooms, strategically placed for the refreshment of tourists. One garden, Hawkestone in Shropshire, even pandered to the tourist's taste for the exotic by providing an attendant dressed as a druid, and a resident decrepit hermit who would emerge from his 'cave' muttering 'Memento mori' and waving two bloody stumps at surprised – not to say appalled – visitors.

Gardens of the first half of the eighteenth century depended for their success on the interaction of observer and creator. For Walpole, Stowe conjured up the ghosts of the personalities commemorated and involved in its creation: 'All these images crowd upon one's memory, and add visionary personages to the charming scenes, that are so enriched with fanes and temples, that the real prospects are little less than visions themselves.'[23] Stowe, like its contemporaries, was primarily a landscape of association, deliberately evoking literary and philosophical ideas by

The Rev. Gilbert White, author of *The Natural History and Antiquities of Selborne*, had a hermitage built in the 1750s on the hill behind his house, The Wakes, at Selborne in Hampshire. His brother Harry, also a vicar, entertained guests by dressing up as the hermit, as shown in this watercolour painted by the Swiss artist, Samuel Hieronymus Grimm, in 1777.

the use of inscriptions and monuments, and demonstrating a favourite theme of Latin poets: the identification of a man's estate with its owner. For these associations to work, an observer was needed to make the connection, thus confirming both the status of the garden's creator as a man of culture and taste, and the outsider's own intellectual ability to recognise the allusions. So, when Henry Hoare placed a statue of the river-god Tiber in his grotto at Stourhead, pointing to the Pantheon on the hill above him, he was offering the visitor a chance to engage in an intellectual game, appreciating the references to Aeneas and ancient Rome, and at the same time making the connection between the Trojan as begetter of a dynasty of Roman emperors and Hoare himself as founder of another 'empire' at Stourhead.

At the same time, gardens like Stowe and Stourhead operated on a visual level. In addition to the references to classical and contemporary literature, they worked as a series of pictures, drawing the spectator in to marvel at paintings in wood, stone and water. Hoare predicted that his pleasure gardens would be 'a charm[in]g Gasp[ar] picture', following Addison's oft-quoted dictum that 'a man could make a pretty Landskip of his own possessions'. Walpole, describing Hagley to a friend in September 1753, mentioned the hermitage 'so exactly like those in Sadeler's prints', and a 'pretty well under a wood, like the Samaritan woman's in a picture by Nicolo Poussin!'[24] The Grand Tour had provided gentry and nobility with an opportunity to see for themselves the ruined temples in the Roman Campagna. Claude's carefully composed views of these scenes hung on the walls of their houses, and their gardens, with their pre-defined viewing points framed by trees, with temples in the middle ground, were real-life attempts to recreate the landscapes of Claude or Poussin or Salvator Rosa. Here too, the garden was an opportunity for the interaction of observer and creator, a deliberate invitation to tourists to respond.

And respond they certainly did. To take just one example, Stourhead was one of the most popular of English gardens after Henry Hoare opened it to visitors of all classes in the 1740s:

> Prepare the mind for something grand and new;
> For Paradise soon opens to the view! ...
> The wond'ring rustics, who this place explore,
> Feel sentiments their souls ne'er felt before;
> And Virtuosi with amazement own
> They never thought such wonders were in stone![25]

Twenty-five years later its popularity caused Mrs Lybbe Powys an unexpected problem: 'We intended laying at the inn at Stourton, built by Mr Hoare for the company that comes to see his place, but to our great mortification, when we got there at near ten o'clock, it was full, and we were obliged to go on to Mere.'[26] Undeterred, she and her party returned the next day, when the gardens 'answered every difficulty we had met with the preceding evening, as both house and grounds are so vastly well worth seeing'.

The river-god Tiber sitting in his grotto at Stourhead, indicating the Pantheon on the hill above. Like the monuments at Stowe, he is part of a complex message being proffered to the visitor. In this case the onlooker is reminded that Aeneas founded the Roman Empire, while Henry Hoare was the founder of an 'empire' at Stourhead.

Left: *An Architectural Capriccio in the Manner of Panini* by Francis Harding. This hangs in the Column Room at Stourhead along with watercolour views of Rome and the surrounding countryside. It shows the kind of monuments that were reproduced in the landscape gardens of eighteenth-century English gentlemen. The pyramid theme in the left background was adopted for the Mausoleum in the grounds of Blickling (*above*), commissioned in 1794 from Joseph Bonomi to receive the remains of the 2nd Earl of Buckinghamshire and his two countesses.

Of course it would be easy to overestimate the extent to which Stourhead, or Hagley, or any of the other great gardens of the eighteenth century, were actually perceived by the mass of visitors as their owners intended. Association and the resulting enhancement of status may have been one of the motivating forces behind their creation, but for most tourists, the fact that a garden was there, was famous and had lots to see was probably quite enough to make a visit worthwhile.

Parallel with the fascination for the classical was a continuing antiquarian interest in the Gothic. The Society of Antiquaries, which had flourished briefly during the last years of the sixteenth century, was reformed in 1707, with the object of studying all relics of British culture pre-dating the reign of James I. Several provincial societies soon followed, notably Spalding, Peterborough, Stamford, Lincoln and Worcester. Nor was dry antiquarian curiosity the only response to medieval architecture. Guy Miége, in *The New State of England* (1691), exhibited an explicitly aesthetic reaction to several Gothic cathedrals: Lincoln he thought 'one of the stateliest piles in England'; while Salisbury was 'indeed one of the principal ornaments of England … a most stately and magnificent church'[27] – sentiments that find an echo in Defoe's remarks on Lichfield Cathedral: 'One of the finest and most beautiful in England, especially for the outside, the form and figure of the building, the carv'd work'd, imagery, and the three beautiful spires; the like of which are not to be seen in one church, no not in Europe.'[28]

It is clear that at a time when Gothic architecture was rejected by virtually all of the leading architectural theorists of the day, attitudes among amateurs were much more ambivalent, much more diverse than one might expect. One can even find emotional responses to the buildings of the past: at Malmesbury Abbey in Wiltshire in 1678, Anthony à Wood confessed to feeling 'a strange veneration come upon me to see the ruins of such a majestic and gigantic pile',[29] while fifty years later the printer and topographer Thomas Gent described his feelings on visiting Kirkstall Abbey in Yorkshire: 'I left my horse at a stile; and passing over it, came down, by a gentle descent, towards its awful ruins; which, Good God! were enough to strike the most harden'd heart, into the softest and most serious reflexion.'[30] In Gent's account of this visit, an admiration of the aesthetics of the Gothic is supplemented by awe and wonder, amounting almost to an embryonic Romantic sensibility of the sort that was to become commonplace among tourists by the beginning of the nineteenth century.

This interest in the architecture of the past extended to more recent buildings during the early years of the eighteenth century. The associations with Charles II made Boscobel in Shropshire, with its Royal Oak, an attraction from the Restoration onwards. By the 1750s it was an established landmark:

> They show, up in the garret, the trap door by which the king went down and sat in an enclosed place … We were then conducted to the site of the Oak. Close to it is an oak about 70 or 80 years old, which they rose up from an acorn of the tree; up on a bough of that tree the king was hid, or in the

hollow of it the king was hid, when they were searching for him in the house. The tree is enclosed with a wall.[31]

Visiting Ditchley in Oxfordshire, once the seat of Queen Elizabeth's champion, Sir Henry Lee, in 1718, Thomas Hearne thought that 'this old house is a very notable thing, and I think I was never better pleased with any sight whatsoever than with this house, which hath been the seat of persons of true loyalty and virtue'.[32]

However, opinions on Elizabethan architecture varied. 'Vast rooms, no taste', wrote Horace Walpole in his journal after a visit to Hardwick Hall in 1760. He elaborated this view in a letter to George Montagu: 'Never was I less charmed in my life. The house is not Gothic, but of that betweenity, that intervened when Gothic declined and Palladian was creeping in – rather, this is totally naked of either. It has vast chambers, aye, vast, such as the nobility of that time delighted in and did not know how to furnish.'[33]

At least Walpole managed to distinguish Elizabethan architecture as a building style in its own right, which was more than many of his Georgian contemporaries were capable of doing. For the majority of tourists however, a country house or, indeed, any building, was either old – in which case it may or may not be interesting, depending on its state of decay, its historical associations, its contents – or new. And no matter what it looked like, if it was new, it deserved some comment, even if only a criticism of the builder's lamentable want of taste, since criticism denoted discrimination, and the ability to discriminate was becoming a decided social asset.

If there is one word that provides a keynote for the many and varied responses of the tourist to modern architecture during the first half of the eighteenth century, it is 'taste'. Essays were written on taste; newspapers argued about taste; and everybody strove to exhibit good taste, until an anonymous writer in the 1750s complained: 'The fine ladies and gentleman dress with taste ... the painters paint with taste, and, in short, fiddlers, players, singers, dancers, and mechanics themselves are all the sons and daughters of taste. Yet in this amazing superabundance of taste few can say what it really is, or what the word signifies.'[34]

While philosophers and theoreticians struggled to define exactly what taste was, there were plenty of commentators who were more than happy to point out examples of both good and bad taste. The baroque, for example, was very definitely bad taste by the middle of the eighteenth century. Visiting Blenheim on 17 July 1760, Walpole dismissed Vanbrugh's work as 'execrable within, without, & almost all round'.[35] Pope, in the famous 'Epistle to the Earl of Burlington, of the use of riches', which first appeared in 1732, poured scorn on the archetypal baroque mansion as exemplified by Timon's villa, which was widely taken at the time to be modelled on the Duke of Chandos's Canons in Middlesex:

> the chapel's silver bell you hear,
> That summons you to all the pride of prayer ...

Left: Congreve's Monument, designed by William Kent for Lord Cobham's landscape garden at Stowe. Cobham had the monument erected in 1736 in memory of the dramatist William Congreve, fellow member and drinking companion of the Whig fraternity, the Kit-Cat Club. At the top of the monument sits a monkey gazing at himself in the mirror, with an inscription that translates from the Latin as 'Comedy is the Imitation of Life, and the Glass of Fashion'.

Above: Sir Thomas Gresham, sixteenth-century founder of the Royal Exchange in London, leads the procession of British Worthies in their Temple at Stowe. Designed by William Kent, it is a statement of Lord Cobham's opposition to the politics of Robert Walpole, with sixteen busts of Immortal Britons, half from the realm of Ideas and half from the field of Action. The only female is that Woman of Action, Queen Elizabeth I.

> On painted ceilings you devoutly stare,
> Where sprawl the saints of Verrio or Laguerre.[36]

In the dining-chamber:

> The rich buffet well-coloured serpents grace,
> And gaping Tritons spew to wash your face.
> Is this a dinner? this a genial room?
> No, 'tis a temple, and a hecatomb.
> A solemn sacrifice, performed in state,
> You drink by measure, and to minutes eat.[37]

Less than ten years before, Defoe had written of Canons as 'the most magnificent [house] in England', and had declared approvingly: 'No nobleman in England, and very few in Europe, lives in greater splendour, or maintains a grandeur and magnificence, equal to the Duke of Chandos.'[38] But now pride, opulence and display for its own sake were roundly condemned, and Pope went on to make the familiar call for function rather than show: ''Tis use alone that sanctifies expense,/And splendour borrows all her rays from sense.'[39] He was of course reacting against an already fading architectural tradition in the baroque, and advocating the up-to-date building style of Burlington, Kent, Colen Campbell and the Palladians.

It was the Palladians who really shaped the building boom of the early eighteenth century. With the advantage of a stable government, a stable economy and a stable society, a new generation of fiercely nationalistic Whigs rejected the baroque as too foreign, too authoritarian, too closely bound up with Stuart court taste. Seeking a break with the architectural conventions of the past, they found their solution in antiquity, as interpreted by Andrea Palladio and – most importantly – as sanctified by an Englishman, Inigo Jones.

The new movement dates from 1715, when the first volumes of two architectural works appeared: Leoni's translation of Palladio's *I quattro libri dell'architettura*, and Colen Campbell's *Vitruvius Britannicus*, which contained one hundred engravings of classical buildings in Britain. Campbell condemned baroque buildings uncompromisingly – 'The parts are without proportion, solids without their true bearing, heaps of materials without strength, excessive ornaments without grace, and the whole without symmetry'[40] – and the leaders of fashion were quick to accept his views on modern architecture: a steady flow of houses conforming to his own interpretation of classicism appeared during the first fifty years of the eighteenth century. Campbell's Wanstead, Stourhead, Houghton and Mereworth, Lord Burlington's Chiswick, William Kent's Holkham, and their many, many imitators, all grew out of an essentially neo-classical, albeit Palladian, tradition, which demanded that a house should conform to certain commonly held criteria. Colen Campbell's implied virtues – proportion, grace, symmetry and an absence of excessive ornament – were to be the defining factors in English

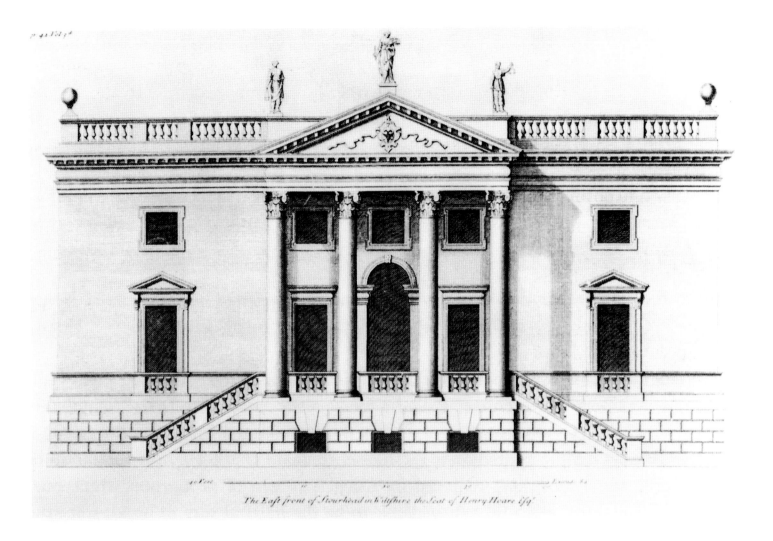

The East front of Stourhead in Wiltshire the Seat of Henry Hoare Esq.

country-house architecture for the next fifty years. The rule of taste had arrived.

To judge from the writings of the Palladians, who were adept at self-advertisement, it would be easy to picture England as a sort of Elysium, characterised in architecture and the fine arts by order, symmetry and proportion, a land overflowing with neo-classical houses, their halls full of antique sculpture and their galleries lined with the works of Claude and Poussin. But the truth is much more complicated. The medieval manor house, the Elizabethan mansion and the ornate baroque palace all still existed, as did the tapestried halls and the galleries full of fading portraits, and they were still valued, if only by a few eccentric cognoscenti. However, the framework within which the consumers of art-objects operated – owner, guest and tourist – was changing dramatically. In an age obsessed with definition and rational analysis, attitudes towards art and architec-

The East Front at Stourhead, from Colen Campbell's *Vitruvius Britannicus*, 1725.

A view in watercolour of Stourhead Landscape Garden by Copplestone Warre Bampfylde, 1775. The artist, a close friend of Henry Hoare, shows the Pantheon on the far side of the lake, the Palladian Bridge in the foreground, the Temple of Apollo on top of the hill on the left, and visitors taking the circular walk.

ture were becoming codified. An understanding of this code and an ability to apply it in discussing a painting or a house were becoming prerequisites for belonging to the upper strata of society. At the same time this concept was filtering down to a growing professional class – Walpole's 'middling sort' – who, far from resenting their social superiors, espoused and aspired to their values and beliefs, and who made up a large proportion of tourists by the middle of the eighteenth century.

As a result, taste, the ability to display informed value-judgements about art and architecture – 'that faculty or those faculties of the mind, which are affected with, or which form a judgment of, the works of imagination and the elegant arts', to use Edmund Burke's definition[41] – was a social indicator. If one really wanted to insult a person, one criticised their taste, as the Earl of Oxford did after visiting Robert Walpole's new house at Houghton in 1722:

> I think it neither magnificent or beautiful. There is a very great expense without either judgement or taste ... I dare say had the money which has been laid out here, nay and much less, been put into the hands of a man of taste and understanding there would have been a much finer house, and better rooms and greater.[42]

The Earl was hardly an impartial observer, of course; he and Walpole were personal enemies, and at opposite ends of the political spectrum. But the mere fact that he chose to denigrate Walpole's taste, that the architecture of a man's house could reflect on his character, demonstrates the importance attached to that faculty by the first quarter of the eighteenth century. The desire and the ability to make coherent and detailed aesthetic judgements was coming to be part of the educated gentleman's and gentlewoman's lifestyle in a way which would have been unfamiliar, even incomprehensible, to their grandparents and great-grandparents.

Not everybody espoused neo-classical ideals – or neo-classical architecture – as wholeheartedly as Pope and Burlington. Typical of contemporary criticisms of Palladianism is Lord Hervey's epigram on Burlington's villa at Chiswick:

> Possessed of one great hall of state,
> Without a room to sleep or eat,
> How well you build let flattery tell,
> And all mankind how ill you dwell.[43]

For many, the idea of trying to reproduce Italian building styles in an English climate was absurd:

> Is there a portal, colonnade, or dome,
> The pride of Naples, or the boast of Rome?
> We raise it here, in storms of wind and hail,
> On the bleak bosom of a sunless vale;
> Careless alike of climate, soil and place,

> The cast of Nature, and the smiles of Grace.
> Hence all our stucco'd walls, mosaic floors,
> Palladian windows, and Venetian doors.[44]

But even among those who scorned Palladianism and the philosophy of neo-classicism which tended to accompany it, the idea of right thinking in matters of taste stuck. Burke, whose *Philosophical Enquiry into the Origin of our Ideas of the Sublime and the Beautiful* (1757) was enormously influential in providing polite society with a sophisticated apparatus for the evaluation of art, architecture and natural scenery, rejected the contemporary infatuation with modernity. His eclectic tastes were well summed up in a letter to the Duke of Dorset:

> I who am something of a lover of all antiquities must be a very great admirer of Knole. I think it the most interesting thing in England. It is pleasant to have preserved in one place the succession of the several tastes of ages; a pleasant habitation for the time, a grand repository of whatever has been pleasant at all times. This is not the sort of place which every banker, contractor, or nabob can create at his pleasure. I am astonished to find so many of your rank of so bad a taste as to give up what distinguishes them, and to adopt what so many can do as well or better than they. I would not change Knole if I were the D of Dorset for all the foppish structures of this enlightened age.[45]

Such praise of an old property as a house, rather than as a monument to the past, was rare indeed. But Burke went further, in rejecting the rationalism of the neo-classicists. 'It is one thing to make an idea clear, and another to make it affecting to the imagination', he wrote in the *Philosophical Enquiry*. 'A clear idea is . . . another name for a little idea.'[46] His emphasis on the importance of an emotional reaction to both art and nature, rather than an intellectual one, gave a certain legitimacy to subjective responses, while his definition of the beautiful and the sublime affected thinking on aesthetics for the next fifty years:

> Sublime objects are vast in their dimensions, beautiful ones comparatively small: beauty should be smooth and polished; the great, rugged and negligent: beauty should shun the right line, yet deviate from it insensibly; the great in many cases loves the right line, and when it deviates it often makes a strong deviation: beauty should not be obscure; the great ought to be dark and gloomy: beauty should be light and delicate; the great ought to be solid, and even massive. They are indeed ideas of a very different nature, one being founded on pain, the other on pleasure.[47]

The beautiful and the sublime were two separate aesthetic modes, and tourists sought them, and distinguished between them, for the rest of the century. Yet even Burke saw the appreciation of art and architecture in terms of rigid criteria: it may be explained in terms of the emotional response of the beholder rather than a cerebral understanding of qualities inherent in the object, but there are still rules. In his essay 'On Taste', he argued that good taste is 'a rectitude of judgement in the arts' and that 'the cause of a wrong taste is a defect of judgement', which usually arises from 'a want of proper and well-directed exercise'. Knowing the right things, and getting in plenty of practice, allow one to 'attain not only a soundness, but a readiness of judgement, as men do by the same methods on all other occasions'.[48] And, following Burke, the tourist in the 1760s saw the experience of country houses, their gardens and their contents as rather more than Celia Fiennes's opportunity for a 'change of air and exercise': it was a chance to develop – and to exhibit – one's taste.

CHAPTER 4

The Polite Tourist

I am tormented all day and every day by people that come to
see my house, and have no enjoyment of it in summer. It
would be even in vain to say that the plague was here. I
remember such a report in London when I was a child, and
my uncle Lord Townshend, then secretary of state, was
forced to send guards to keep off the crowd from the house in
which the plague was said to be – they would go and see the
plague. Had I been master of the house, I should have said . . .
'You see the plague! you *are* the plague.'

Horace Walpole to Sir Horace Mann, 30 July 1783[1]

THE 'PLAGUE' was not confined to Walpole's Gothic villa at Strawberry Hill. It
spread rapidly across the country during the late eighteenth century, as polite society, armed with the critical apparatus supplied by Burke's *Philosophical Enquiry*, its
appetite whetted by printed topographical views and published tours and travel
journals, chased through every county in pursuit of culture, antiquity and romance.

Norfolk, with its parade of great houses – Houghton and Holkham, Blickling
and Oxburgh and Raynham – drew the crowds, as did Derbyshire, where visits to
Chatsworth, Hardwick and Kedleston provided light relief for the tourist who
had come to thrill at the scenic grandeur of the Peak and the awfully sublime
caverns of Elden Hole and Speedwell. The south of England had Wilton, of
course, with Wardour Castle, Longford and Stonehenge as obligatory excursions
from a base at Salisbury. In the west, Longleat, Stourhead, Mount Edgecumbe
and Saltram were all popular. Due largely to Henry Penruddocke Wyndham's *A
Gentleman's Tour through Monmouthshire and Wales in June and July 1774*, the tour of
Wales was steadily gaining in popularity, as the romantic appeal of that country's
castles and abbeys became more widely appreciated. In fact, virtually every part of
the kingdom found that its art and architecture, hitherto neglected, or admired
only by a select band of dilettanti, was in demand.

Inevitably, this put a certain amount of pressure on the owners of country
houses. It is impossible to guess how many tourists turned up at particular properties – very few reliable figures are available. But statistics are scattered around here
and there, in journals, diaries and visitors' books. Mrs Lybbe Powys in 1776
observed that 'few persons pass by Wilton, as in the porter's lodge, where he
desired us to set down our names and the number of our company, we saw by the

book there had been to see it the last year 2,324 persons'.[2] The detailed lists of visitors kept at Strawberry Hill between 1784 and 1797 show that around 300 people a year came to see the house between May and the end of September, when it was officially open. 'My house is a torment, not a comfort!' exclaimed Walpole in June 1786, after three German barons had arrived on his doorstep just as he was about to dine.[3] And on a number of occasions he was reduced to hiding in his bed-chamber while his housekeeper showed parties round.

Awkward situations like this were bound to occur, as an activity which had been confined to a few dedicated amateurs was taken up by relatively large numbers. In the past, allowing access to one's home and collections had grown up within the secure framework provided by medieval conventions of hospitality and good housekeeping, it was becoming obvious by the 1770s that such an informal approach would have to be modified, as the craze for country house visiting grew. The strictly graduated society of the seventeenth century, the absolutist model which had expressed itself in great baroque palaces like Versailles and Blenheim, was no longer acceptable to most educated people, and the propertied classes demanded a social parity that would have been unthinkable one hundred years before:

> The polite world saw themselves as an elite, whose claim to run the country was based on having a stake in it as property owners, and was reinforced by the culture, education and *savoir-faire* of which its country houses were an advertisement. The monarch was the head of government, but his powers were defined and restricted, and derived from consent not right. The nobility were given the respect due to major and long-established property owners, but not the reverence due to gods in miniature. The members of the property-owning elite moved among themselves with relative equality.[4]

In architecture, this was reflected in the appearance of the compact Palladian villa: the baroque sequence of state rooms, each one more exclusive than the last, was rejected in favour of a circuit of connected chambers through which all members of the collective elite could move and mingle in comparative freedom. In town planning, the old centralised layout, with a palace at the junction of a series of avenues – vistas radiating out from the centre – was being superseded by a grouping of several focal points, as at Bath, where Assembly Rooms, Pump Rooms, Abbey and the various baths were linked together by a series of terraces, again forming an informal circuit through which the upper classes could stroll and socialise. And in the relaxed pastime of country-house visiting, this shift in attitude among the gentry and professional classes led not only to a demand to participate in polite activities (among which the appreciation of art and architecture played an important role), but also to an assumption of social equality which the aristocracy found threatening and unsettling.

The experience of an MP's wife, Lady Beauchamp Proctor, demonstrates perfectly the widening gulf between what the visitor expected of his or her 'host', and what that host was prepared to suffer in opening his house to the genteel

In 1747 Horace Walpole bought Strawberry Hill near Twickenham, on the banks of the Thames, describing it as 'the prettiest bauble you ever saw'. For the next fifty years he extended the small house, fitting it out in the Gothic style and filling it with his collections. This engraving, from *A Description of the Villa* published in 1784, shows the Tribune where Walpole kept all his best treasures. In the centre of the alcove is a cabinet he designed, which contained his fine collection of miniatures.

One of the houses on the Norfolk circuit for eighteenth-century visitors: Blickling Hall, home of the Hobarts since the early seventeenth century.

public. Arriving at the Earl of Buckinghamshire's Blickling in September 1772, Lady Beauchamp Proctor noted that 'My Lord's horses stood at the door, though the servant told us he was gone out. We saw no other traces of her Ladyship than two or three workbags and a tambour; I believe we drove her from room to room, but that we couldn't help.' After being conducted through the house, the party was about to leave when the Earl appeared, and 'made a thousand courtier-like speeches, but they were so little worth attending to that they went in at one ear and out at t'other; one thing, however, I could not help remarking – he said he was mortified beyond expression that he happened to be out when we came, and you know I have mentioned his horses being at the door when we went in.'[5]

A reform of visiting arrangements at the most popular houses was obviously necessary – and it was not simply a matter of social inconvenience. While many tourists expected to be treated as guests, their behaviour often left a great deal to be desired. Lady Beauchamp Proctor gaily admitted that at Wolterton in Norfolk she poked some delicate frescoes with her stick to reassure herself that they weren't mere stucco-work.[6] But this pales in comparison with the numerous acts of theft and vandalism which were becoming commonplace at houses that regularly opened their doors to the public. Philip Southcote was forced to close his gardens at Wooburn Farm near Weybridge, after 'savages, who came as connoisseurs, scribbled a thousand brutalities in the buildings.'[7] At Blenheim, a set of Meissen presented to the Duke of Marlborough by the King of Poland had to be kept under lock and key because so many pieces had been broken by tourists, while any number of small items, including a miniature worth five hundred guineas, had simply vanished.

It is scarcely surprising that some owners did in fact put all thoughts of duty and *noblesse oblige* behind them, and closed their doors. Tourists, sometimes travelling miles out of their route only to be turned away, reacted in different ways. Robert Clutterbuck, failing to gain admission to Lord Lisburne's Mamhead in Devon during a tour of the western counties in the summer of 1796, took the news quite philosophically: 'We were not permitted to see the interior of the house; whether it contained nothing worthy of inspection, or whether the sight of it is attended with inconvenience to the present Lord who is advanced in years; but we were inclined to assign the last reason.'[8] On the other hand, John Byng, a retired army officer working for the Inland Revenue at Somerset House who was also an inveterate tourist, was not so charitable when he was turned away from Shirburn Castle in Oxfordshire: 'Let people proclaim that their great houses are not to be view'd, and then travellers will not ride out of their way with false hopes.' He went on to vent his spleen on the castle itself: 'This appears to be a very ugly place, in a very ugly country ... and the whole appearance is melancholy and tasteless.'[9]

Byng's anger and disappointment are partly explained by the fact that this was the second time within a few days that he had been refused admission to a country house. At Wroxton, also in Oxfordshire, where Lord Guilford was in residence, he exclaimed, 'Let him either forbid his place entirely; open it always; or else fix a

day of admission.'[10] And it was this last option that began to appeal to a number of owners. As early as 1760, Chatsworth was open on two 'public' days only each week. By the 1790s, other owners had followed the Duke of Devonshire's example: Blenheim was open from two till four; Woburn Abbey in Bedfordshire on Mondays only; and Beckford's Fonthill Splendens in Wiltshire every day from twelve to four. In general, information on opening hours was available at local inns and in neighbouring towns. The old man who showed Richard Sulivan around Derby in 1778 was quick to point out that their party must hurry to nearby Kedleston Hall if they were to see it that day: 'Our old Cicerone, stopping and looking at the sun, cried, "Come, come, gentlemen, if you have a mind to see Lord Scarsdale's, you must go directly; it is now noon, and travellers have no admittance but from ten till two."'[11] And, of course, printed journals like Sulivan's were widely read by aspiring tourists, so that the necessary information was publicised, to a certain extent at least, at a national level.

A more radical step towards placing country-house visiting on a formal basis was the issuing in advance of tickets, often with a set of rules attached. From the 1770s onwards, for example, Horace Walpole would only allow his housekeeper to admit visitors to Strawberry Hill if they were able to show her a signed ticket obtained from him. In the early days of the villa's popularity, this usually took the form of a written note, although in 1774 Walpole printed his own cards on which were inserted the date of the proposed visit and his signature. By 1784 he was issuing a 'page of rules for admission to see my house', at the bottom of which he would write a note to his housekeeper, mentioning the name of the applicant and the number in the party, as well as the date of the visit:

> Mr Walpole is very ready to oblige any curious persons with the sight of his house and collection; but as it is situated so near to London and in so populous a neighbourhood, and as he refuses a ticket to nobody that sends for one, it is but reasonable that such persons as send, should comply with the rules he has been obliged to lay down for showing it.

> Any person, sending a day or two before, may have a ticket for four persons for a day certain.

> No ticket will serve but on the day for which it is given. If more than four persons come with a ticket, the housekeeper has positive orders to admit none of them.

> Every ticket will admit the company only between the hours of twelve and three before dinner, and only one company will be admitted on the same day.

> The house will never be shown after dinner; nor at all but from the first of May to the first of October.

The Gothic Library at Strawberry Hill. The painted ceiling was designed by Horace Walpole himself, and features two of his Crusader ancestors, while the bookcases were the creation of his friend, John Chute of The Vyne. The chimneypiece was an amalgam of the tomb of John of Eltham in Westminster Abbey, and of that of Thomas, Duke of Clarence, at Canterbury Cathedral.

As Mr Walpole has given offence by sometimes enlarging the number of four, and refusing that latitude to others, he flatters himself that for the future nobody will take it ill that he strictly confines the number; as whoever desires him to break his rule, does in effect expect him to disoblige others, which is what nobody has a right to desire him.

Persons desiring a ticket, may apply either to Strawberry Hill, or to Mr Walpole's in Berkeley Square, London. If any person does not make use of the ticket, Mr Walpole hopes he shall have notice; otherwise he is prevented from obliging others on that day, and thence is put to great inconvenience.

They that would have tickets are desired not to bring children.[12]

Such well-defined and formalised regulations were still the exception rather than the rule, and Walpole's letters show that he was prepared to waive them all (except for the ban on children) as circumstances dictated.

At the same time, the public was demanding not only the right of entry to country houses, but a more authoritative and comprehensive account of their contents than a housekeeper could be expected to provide. We have seen that touring was no longer the sole prerogative of connoisseurs and antiquarians, reasonably well-equipped to form their own judgements and to compare and contrast individual works of art. The new breed of visitor, the polite tourist, now aspired to that status – indeed, one of the reasons for making the round of country houses and gardens was to develop one's taste and to refine one's sensibilities. To cater for this thirst for knowledge, catalogues and guidebooks to individual properties began to make their appearance towards the end of the eighteenth century. Expensively produced commemorative volumes, intended for the gentleman's library rather than for practical use, had appeared here and there as early as the 1730s and 1740s. *Aedes Walpolianae, or a Description of the Collection of Pictures at Houghton Hall in Norfolk* is typical. Called a 'plain description of the effects', it provided a catalogue of the 260-plus paintings, bronzes and busts on show, together with two folding plans and elevations, Horace Walpole's 'Sermon on Painting', and Whaley's poem, 'A Journey to Houghton'.[13] But it was not a guide-book in the modern sense – its size and price ensured that it was bought by the discerning dilettante rather than the casual tourist, while the works of art were dealt with in a 'critical order' which differed considerably from the order in which they were shown.

By the middle of the century, however, a few enterprising booksellers, stationers and engravers were publishing modestly priced guides to the main tourist attractions. Benton Seeley's *A Description of the House and Gardens ... at Stow*, which first appeared in 1744, went through some twenty-two editions in fifty years, in spite of competition from George Bickham's *The Beauties of Stow*, the 1750 edition of which could be bought at 'Mr Hoskins at the New Inn going into the gardens' for four shillings. (Seeley's 1756 *Description* could be obtained for a

The title page of the guidebook to
Wilton House, published in 1751.

more modest price: sixpence for the basic guide, a shilling if a plan was included, and five shillings for the deluxe edition bound, with a series of views.)

It would be misleading to suggest that any but the largest and most prestigious houses had moved towards a formalised system of coping with visitors by the end of the century. No more than perhaps fifteen or twenty properties were the subject of individual catalogues. These were the great houses on the major tourist routes: Houghton, Holkham, Stowe, Blenheim (where William Mavor's *New Description* was also available in French) and Wilton (which could also boast a foreign-language guide, this time in Italian). At the vast majority of houses, visitors were received – or turned away – on the same basis as they had been in the past. But now there were more of them. They tended to be more critical, if not more discriminating. And their expectations were high.

The day of 7 June 1789 was a clear, windy Sunday. For John Byng, it was the tenth day of a summer excursion through the Midlands. Each year it was Byng's habit to spend June and July travelling through various parts of England and Wales, examining and sketching churches, hunting for old castles and visiting the various country houses which he came across on his route. In 1789, after a leisurely ride up from London, he had arrived in Grantham, where he spent a few hours before going over to look at Belvoir Castle in Leicestershire, the seat of the eleven-year-old John Henry Manners, fifth Duke of Rutland. 'When we approached the Belvoir Stables, we enquired for an inn (for my wish is for a noon stop at a quiet inn, and there to eat of the family dinner), and were directed to the Peacock, a house of the proper sort; here they spoke of a leg of mutton to be ready in an hour, one o'clock.'[14] Byng and his friend then walked up the steep hill to the castle entrance, where they gave their names and asked to be admitted. 'The housekeeper soon came; of a very drunken, dawdling appearance', and conducted them round the seventeenth-century house, showing them through the various state rooms and the 'old shabby chapel . . . disused to prayers', and pointing out the most notable pieces of furniture and the best paintings. Her mistakes and misattributions, says Byng, 'were numberless, – pointing to a picture of the great Duke of Buckingham, she call'd him that villain Felton; finely confusing the murder'd with the murderer!'

Notwithstanding the housekeeper's errors, Byng was impressed with the collections at Belvoir, commenting favourably on the Reynolds and the Gainsboroughs, the Rubens and the Murillos, and the 'most superb collection of ancient portraits'. But he was no connoisseur; a practical, down-to-earth type of man, he was angered by the late Duke's order of priorities:

> There is no furniture (pictures excepted) that a broker would think worth the carrying away . . . I think that fine pictures are a beautiful addition to the elegancies of life; but when I see the walls of great rooms cover'd by valuable paintings, and at the same time wanting good chairs, tables, grates, curtains, and carpets, I condemn such mistaken pride and folly!

A

DESCRIPTION

OF THE

PICTURES, STATUES, BUSTO's
BASSO-RELIEVO's,

AND OTHER

CURIOSITIES

AT THE

Earl of PEMBROKE's House

AT

WILTON.

The Antiques of this Collection contain
the whole of Cardinal RICHLIEU's and Cardinal MAZARINE's, and the greatest Part
of the Earl of ARUNDEL's; besides several
particular Pieces purchased at different Times.

By RICHARD COWDRY.

L O N D O N:
Printed for the Author, and sold by J. ROBINSON, at
the *Golden Lion,* in *Ludgate-Street*; at Mr. LEAKE's,
at *Bath,* and at Mr. GIBBS's Glover, at *Salisbury*.

MDCCLI.

And after spending ninety minutes touring Belvoir, his final verdict was: 'One night's losings at play of the late duke had furnish'd this house: at present there is not an habitable room, or a bed fit to sleep in.' With that, he returned down the hill to the Peacock and his 'family dinner' of roast mutton, rice-pudding and gooseberry pie.

Byng's experience of the practical business of viewing a country house in the later eighteenth century is typical, even if his opinions are rather more forthright than most. One can see it repeated in that most famous of all country-house visits, Elizabeth Bennett's tour of Pemberley in *Pride and Prejudice*. Like John Byng, Elizabeth and her aunt and uncle are shown round by the housekeeper, Mrs Reynolds, who relates 'the subjects of the pictures, the dimensions of the rooms, and the price of the furniture'; unlike Byng, she approves of what she sees: 'The rooms were lofty and handsome, and their furniture suitable to the fortune of their proprietor; but Elizabeth saw, with admiration of his taste, that it was neither gaudy nor uselessly fine.' But then Belvoir Castle didn't have a Darcy – and even if it did, one has the impression that crusty old Byng would have dismissed him as an arrogant fop.

So, in spite of the process of formalisation that was being forced upon some of the more popular houses by an increasing number of tourists, the procedure generally remained the same: one sent a servant ahead to enquire if it would be convenient to see the place, or gave in one's card at the porter's lodge, or simply knocked at the door and asked to come in. Even at the major houses, where fixed opening hours had been introduced, this was still the accepted procedure, the only difference being that the servants who showed you round would expect a more substantial tip.

It was usually the housekeeper's job to give guided tours of a house – quite a lucrative occupation, at between one shilling and half-a-crown a time. Horace Walpole, writing to the Countess of Ossory in 1783, declared that his housekeeper, Margaret, obtained such sums of money from showing Strawberry Hill, 'that I have a mind to marry her, and so repay myself that way for what I have flung away to make my house quite uncomfortable to me'.[15] Not surprisingly, the tourist usually took a less sanguine point of view. One Irish cleric, after visiting Blenheim (whose servants had a notorious reputation for exploiting tourists), complained that he and his companions were virtually destitute, 'having our pockets egregiously picked by those beggarly and rascally conductors not only here but in all the places of public resort where strangers in England generally go to gratify their curiosity'.[16]

Very occasionally, the tourist might be fortunate enough to be shown over the house by the owner himself. Such was Richard Sulivan's experience at an elegant mansion a few miles from Birmingham, where 'Doctor B——y, the gentleman unto whom it belongs' conducted Sulivan's party through every apartment, and even pressed them to take some refreshment with him. The delighted tourist was quite overwhelmed: 'Hail! gentle courtesy; thou fairest born of sweet benevolence!

How kindly dost thou cheer the weary traveller on his way! Thy dimpled smile dost beckon us as we journey it along! Thou scatterest roses to the shorn lamb, and warmest the heart that's chilled with sorrow!'[17] Sulivan's lyrical reaction to what might seem an act of simple hospitality is in part explained by the often-noted shortcomings of a system whereby an uneducated, and often illiterate, servant was given the task of lecturing on history and art history to aspiring connoisseurs. 'NB The servant that shewed the house, ignorant and insolent', scribbled an anonymous visitor to Stowe at the bottom of a long and detailed account of the house and gardens.[18] And there was general agreement that not only were servants in general an ignorant and insolent breed, but that their attitude could make or mar a visit to a country house. 'The manner in which the house is shown', wrote William Bray of Chatsworth, 'does not much prejudice a person in its favour.'[19] Few travellers, however, can have been unfortunate enough to undergo Lady Beauchamp Proctor's experience at Raynham, where the house was shown by 'one old witch and a great dog, that attended us all over the house, and saluted every corner that was convenient for his purposes'.[20]

Perhaps the most striking instance of the freedom with which some guides treated their master's houses comes from Byng, who was shown over another of the Duke of Rutland's properties, the medieval Haddon Hall, by a farmer who rented the old out-buildings:

> 'Sir,' quoth the farmer (my intelligent guide) 'many gentlemen will stay hours in this house, and prefer the observation here to the being in Chatsworth.'
> 'That's just my case.'
> 'And some, Sir, will desire to take away pieces of armour.'
> 'That I shou'd like to do, too.'
> 'Why then, Sir, as you seem fond of these things, there is a sword hilt, with part of the blade, said to be worn by the Vernons in the wars of France;' and so I instantly carried him off.[21]

It was still the relative simplicity of Palladianism and neo-classicism (few visitors distinguished between the two styles), the combination of simplicity and grandeur, that commanded the most admiration, even among travellers who enjoyed exploring old manor houses and castles. If the Middle Ages meant chivalry and romance, then to the aspiring connoisseur classicism meant culture, civilisation and modern comforts. In some ways the climate had not changed so much since the early years of the century. Burlington, Campbell and the other Palladians were still highly thought of. But it was the more recent work of Robert Adam which provoked the most ecstatic exclamations of praise. Adam had travelled extensively in Italy in the 1750s. He had studied classical architecture *in situ*. He knew Piranesi, whose imaginative reconstructions of ancient Rome had done so much to inspire a new attitude towards classical antiquity. And on his return to England in 1758 he quickly established himself as the most sought-after designer

The State Bed at Osterley Park, designed by Robert Adam in the 1770s. When Horace Walpole visited the house in 1773, he was ecstatic in his praise of the architecture, but drew the line at the State Bed, which he found 'too theatric and too like a modern head-dress ... What would Vitruvius think of a dome decorated by a milliner?'

of his generation, introducing a whole new range of classical motifs and room plans and providing grand façades and elegant interiors perfectly suited to the sensibilities of the eighteenth-century connoisseur. At Osterley, remodelled by Adam for the banker Robert Child in the 1760s and 1770s, Horace Walpole grew positively ecstatic:

> On Friday we went to see – oh, the palace of palaces! – and yet a palace sans crown, sans coronet, but such expense! such taste! and such profusion! ... The old house I have often seen, which was built by Sir Thomas Gresham; but it is so improved and enriched, that all the Percies and Seymours of Sion must die of envy. [Adam had worked at Syon House between 1760 and 1769.] There is a double portico that fills the space between the towers of the front, and is as noble as the Propyleum of Athens. There is a hall, library, breakfast-room, eating-room, all chefs-d'oeuvre of Adam, a gallery one hundred and thirty feet long, and a drawing-room worthy of Eve before the fall.[22]

Wherever travellers experienced Adam's creations, his work was admired. But even in the midst of so much acclaim, one building stands out as being perhaps the most consistently praised country house of the period – Kedleston Hall, the 'Glory of Derbyshire'. Kedleston was the seat of Sir Nathaniel Curzon, a wealthy Derbyshire landowner whose Grand Tour had resulted in a fine art collection and a passion for the architecture of ancient Rome. Curzon demolished his early eighteenth-century family home, believing that the neat redbrick house was inappropriate both for the display of his collection, and for the barony which he was working hard to acquire. (He was finally created Baron Scarsdale of Scarsdale in April 1761.) The new north front was begun by James Paine in 1759, but by 1761 Paine had been replaced by Adam, whose synthesis of Roman motifs and traditional Palladian plan provided just the sort of elegant status symbol that Curzon required. The result was described by Richard Warner forty years later:

> The front, which is of white stone, hewn on Lord Scarsdale's estate, divides itself into three parts – a body and two pavilions, connected to the main building by corridors of the Doric order, taking a sweeping form; that on the right (as we approach it) comprising the kitchen and offices, that on the left consisting of Lord Scarsdale's private apartments. In the centre of the front (to the north) is a double flight of steps leading to a grand portico, whose pediment is supported by six pillars of the Corinthian order. From hence is a beautiful home view, embracing the skilful improvements of Lord Scarsdale, whose gigantic plan included the transplanting of a village that stood in front of the house to a distant part.[23]

In the grounds a sulphurous medicinal spring drew the occasional invalid, and, nearby, Curzon had built an inn, 'for the accommodation of such strangers as curiosity may lead to view his residence'.[24]

Above: *The Arch of Constantine in Rome*, a watercolour by Abraham Louis Ducros in the Column Room at Stourhead. Robert Adam used the design of the arch for the centre of the south front at Kedleston (*right*).

And view it they did. 'The most perfect, that I ever saw', wrote one anonymous tourist; 'all is consistent and uniform, and all is in the most elegant style.'[25] 'Of all the houses I ever saw', said William Bray after his visit there in 1777, 'I do not recollect any one which so completely pleased me as this.'[26] And Richard Sulivan was almost beside himself with pleasure at his first sight of the interior:

> You get into a most superb hall, the sides and ceilings of which are the most beautifully ornamented, and the whole supported by four and twenty massive pillars of variegated alabaster finely fluted. Here, indeed, the senses become astonished. The alabaster pillars have a wonderful appearance; the other ornaments, likewise, carry their intrinsic proportion of elegance. In

one word, the whole strikes you as if it were designed for a more than mortal residence ... Altogether this house is really magnificent: the hand of taste is evident in every part of it (nor can it be otherwise, when known to be the work of Messieurs Adam).[27]

Kedleston Hall's popularity with the polite tourist was due to a combination of factors, some unconnected with its architectural merits. Some visitors remarked that 'the uncommon politeness and attention of the person who shewed it, added not a little to the entertainment'.[28] This was Curzon's housekeeper Mrs Garnett, the 'most distinct articulator' who conducted Johnson and Boswell round the house in 1777.[29] Others appreciated the lived-in quality of the apartments, which 'are not reserved for shew alone, but constantly inhabited by the family, and the numerous friends which his Lordship's hospitality invites'.[30] And, of course, the collection itself, with its Rembrandts, Leonardos and Van Dycks, was a major draw. One picture in particular was singled out for praise – *Daniel Interpreting Nebuchadnezzar's Dreams*, then thought to be by Rembrandt, but now attributed to his fellow Dutchman and imitator, Salomon Koninck. Warner described it as 'one of the finest productions of the pencil of Rembrandt ... The solemnity of Daniel's figure; the attention and alarm in the different faces; the grandeur of the

Right: Mrs Garnett, Lord Scarsdale's housekeeper at Kedleston from 1766 to 1809. In this portrait by Thomas Barber she is depicted in the Marble Hall, guidebook in hand, ready to welcome her visitors and take them round the house.

Far right: The Marble Hall at Kedleston. Adam created the feeling of an atrium, or open courtyard of a Roman villa, by running two sets of monumental columns in alabaster down the length of the hall and placing classical statues in niches along the walls.

Daniel before Nebuchadnezzar by the seventeenth-century Dutch artist, Salomon Koninck, hanging in the Library at Kedleston. This picture was particularly admired by eighteenth-century visitors, who thought it the work of Rembrandt.

king; and the splendid light emanating from the mithra, or emblem of the sun, behind the king's throne, are all indications of transcendent genius and skill.'[31] Sulivan, too, was impressed, calling the painting 'a most highly finished picture', although he went on to qualify his praise somewhat by suggesting that 'Daniel's hair, and the apparel in general, is preposterous'.[32]

Sir Nathaniel Curzon had amassed his collection during the 1750s, through agents in Italy and salerooms in London. It contained paintings by seventeenth-century artists like Guercino and Maratta, Giordano and Strozzi, although there were also several more important works, as well as the inevitable portraits by, or after, Lely and Kneller. But while the collection was certainly a major one, at Kedleston, as elsewhere, the polite tourist was by and large content merely to note the pictures that attracted him or her, offering little in the way of critical comment beyond the occasional 'fine' or 'very striking'.

This is not to suggest that visitors were visually illiterate. On the contrary, most were well acquainted with the work of a broad range of artists, and, when the occasion arose, many were capable of making highly individual judgements. As with everything else related to the country house, they were far from slow to express their likes and dislikes. Byng thought that the 'faded pictures by Sir J Reynolds' which he saw at Grimsthorpe in Lincolnshire in 1789 were 'of no value to anyone'; and the Rubens at Blenheim elicited the remark that the artist was 'not a favourite master of mine, as all his male figures are coarse, and his women wet nurses'.[33] At the other end of the critical spectrum, the Revd William MacRitchie had no hesitation in judging Carlo Dolci's *Christ Blessing the Bread*, which he was shown during a visit to Burghley, as 'one of the first paintings in the world';[34] while at the Earl of Radnor's Longford Castle, near Salisbury, Robert Clutterbuck was most impressed by two Claudes:

> The greatest ornament is the Picture Gallery, in which, amongst a very scientific, and choice selection of various masters, are two of Claude, perhaps of the best of his works. The subjects, which are to be admired not less for the classical manner in which they are express'd than for their harmony of colouring, are, one a sunrise, the subject Aeneas landing in Italy, the other a sun setting on the ruins of Rome.[35]

Contemporary English art, with the occasional exception of Reynolds and Gainsborough, is rarely mentioned, although this says more about the nature of the country-house collection at the time than about the predilections of individual tourists. It is Italian art which predominates, from Raphael – 'Over the chimney [at Okeover Hall in Staffordshire], an *Holy Family*, by Raphael, about three feet and a half by two and a half, for which seven thousand guineas have been offered! … The richness of colouring, force, and expression of this picture cannot be spoken of in terms of too high praise'[36] – through Annibale Carracci – 'Of the more Ancient Masters [at Chatsworth] One … which is in higher estimation than any other, *The Flight into Egypt*, by Hannibal Carracci'[37] – and the highly rated late baroque of Carlo Dolci, to near-contemporary neo-classicists such as Anton Raffael Mengs and Pompeo Batoni.

When tourists did respond to native English art, it was in an entirely different way from their reaction to Claude or Raphael:

> [Woburn] is a treasure of paintings; of portraits of the great, now illustrious by the figure they make in the eyes of posterity, undazzled with their wealth, rank, power, or qualifications, mental or corporeal, which concealed their failings, and made them pass at last unnoticed openly by their contemporaries. They now undergo a posthumous trial, and, like the Egyptians of old, receive censure or praise according to their respective merits.[38]

The sight of English portraiture (or, indeed, any portraiture) tended to be seen as an opportunity to hold Thomas Pennant's 'posthumous trial,' provoking reflections on the character of the sitter rather than an analysis of any aesthetic qualities which the painting itself might have possessed. Looking at a picture of Bishop Crewe in the state bed-chamber at Kedleston, Richard Warner commented, 'one of the most despicable characters in the annals of James II'. Cornelius Johnson's portrait of Prince Henry prompted no description, merely the remark that the subject was 'the amiable son of James I whose noble and manly conduct had endeared him to all classes of his father's subjects'.[39] At Blythe Hall in Warwickshire, Pennant, who took a certain delight in pronouncing on the personal failings of the great, was moved by the sight of a half-length of Elias Ashmole to suggest that 'it is well for poor Ashmole, that the peevish historian never read the wonderful diary of his life, in which is a most minute and filthy detail of all his ails and strange mishaps'.[40]

It is no coincidence that Kedleston Hall should have been the most consistently praised of all new houses in the later eighteenth century. It conformed absolutely to the educated classes' conception of what modern architecture ought to be: costly, but not showy; elegant, but not effete; convenient, and in line with the accepted canons of classical taste, but at the same time spectacular enough to stand out from the mass of country houses. Together with its collection, it became a symbol of the ideal: and by noticing and approving of the paintings, the proportions and the grandeur of the whole, tourists could share in the owner's statement of his culture and taste. They were able to demonstrate that they belonged to that collective elite which constituted polite society at the end of the eighteenth century.

CHAPTER 5

Creative Fancy

Hail favour'd casement! where the sight
Is courted to enjoy delight,
T'ascend the hill and trace the plain,
Where lavish Nature's proud to reign!
Unlike those pictures that impart
The windows of Palladian art,
From whence no other object's seen
But gravel walk, or shaven green;
Plann'd by the artist at his desk;
Pictures that are not picturesque.

William Combe,
*Doctor Syntax in Search
of the Picturesque*, 1809[1]

GARDENS LIKE STOURHEAD, Stowe and Rousham in Oxfordshire, were immensely popular with visitors from the middle of the eighteenth century. But it was later in the century that major developments took place in the concept of picturesque landscape, developments which placed the tourist in an active, rather than a passive role. These developments were stimulated by the published writings of William Gilpin, Richard Payne Knight and Uvedale Price.

William Gilpin's tours, most of which were published some years after they had actually been taken, were enormously successful with the public. His *Observations on the River Wye and Several Parts of South Wales ... Relative Chiefly to Picturesque Beauty* went into five editions between its first appearance in 1782 and 1800, when it was also issued in French at Breslau. Tours of Cumberland and Westmorland, the Highlands of Scotland, the New Forest and the West Country followed at intervals throughout the 1780s and 1790s. Gilpin's ideas on the picturesque were not particularly revolutionary: 'Picturesque beauty is a phrase but little understood', he wrote in 1798. 'We precisely mean by it that kind of beauty which would look well in a picture.'[2] He saw landscape in the accepted terms of Claudian composition, defining the characteristics of objects which produced the picturesque as roughness, variety, accident, contrast and ruggedness. But one of Gilpin's most significant contributions to the tourist's critical armoury was the suggestion that it was not necessary to accept passively what one saw on one's travels; it was possible to modify one's experience by using the imagination.

In his essay 'On Picturesque Travel' (1792), Gilpin argued:

> It may perhaps be objected to the pleasurable circumstances, which are ... said to accompany picturesque travel, that we meet as many disgusting, as pleasing objects; and the man of taste therefore will be as often offended, as amused ...
>
> But if we let the imagination loose, even scenes like these, administer great amusement. The imagination can plant hills; can form rivers, and lakes in valleys; can build castles, and abbeys.[3]

The consequences for the tourist were profound. It was the purely visual that characterised much of Gilpin's thought. When, in discussing some Cornish tin mines, he mentioned that he was not interested in going below ground, because 'our business was only on the surface',[4] he was talking about more than mining. And visual perception was no longer a matter of simply looking at a scene and being thrilled by its sublimity, charmed by its beauty or bored by its blandness; it was now acceptable to engage in creative imaginative activity, using a knowledge of art in general, and Claude or Salvator Rosa in particular, to improve on reality.

However, the achievement of such a liberation from the tyranny of the senses could occasionally require a little help. One of the most remarkable aids to the

Below: The Claude Glass, a slightly convex blackened mirror that enabled the Picturesque tourist to create an image of the landscape imbued with the atmosphere of the painter Claude.

Right: Thomas Gainsborough's study of a *Man sketching using a Claude Glass, c.*1750–55.

imagination to find its way into the tourist's saddle-bag was the Claude glass, a plano-convex mirror which reflected a distorted view of the countryside, ready framed and complete with dark foreground features, all tinged with a suitably Claudian blue. For a traveller like Adam Walker, writing in 1791, this little device helped to create an artificial landscape, forcing Nature to conform, for an instant at least, to the tastes and sensibilities of polite society:

> In this fine range of hills (running from Maidenhead Thicket through the long county of Bucks) are situated many elegant seats. We passed one belonging to the Duke of Portland, whose park encloses several of those hills, all clothed with wood in a style worthy the celebrated Brown ... My black mirror presented me with many beautiful landscapes in this park, that a Claude might not have disdained to copy.[5]

The sight of earnest tourists travelling through the Lake District or over the mountains of Wales, pausing here and there to turn away from some of the most sublime scenery in the country so that they could capture its reflection in their Claude glasses, must have been quite a bizarre spectacle. The Curwen family actually went to the lengths of building a small hut on Lake Windermere – Claife Station – which was fitted with variously tinted windows, so that the seeker after picturesque effects could view, through his glass, a landscape by Claude or Salvator Rosa.[6] The taste for different tints also spread to the instruments themselves, which came in a host of pinks, reds and various shades of blue.

But the vogue was relatively short-lived. Already by the end of the 1790s the searcher after the picturesque was being mercilessly lampooned on the stage. 'Where's my Claude-Lorraine?' cries Beccabunga Veronica in James Plumptre's *The Lakers*, as she looks out across Derwentwater to Borrowdale:

> I must throw a Gilpin tint over these magic scenes of beauty. (*Looks through the glass*.) How gorgeously glowing! Now for the darker. (*Looks through the glass*.) How gloomily glaring! Now the blue. (*Pretends to shiver with fright*.) How frigidly frozen! What illusions of vision! The effect is inexpressibly interesting. The amphitheatrical perspective of the long landscape; the peeping points of the many-coloured crags of the head-long mountains, looking out most interestingly from the picturesque luxuriance of the bowery foliage; the delightful differences of the heterogeneous masses; the horrific mountains, such scenes of ruin and privation.[7]

Not content with using her black mirror merely to interpret the landscape of the Lake District, Miss Veronica feels that it may also help her to make sense of her lover: 'I'll throw a Gilpin tint over him. (*Looks through glass*.) Yes, he's gorgeously glowing. I must not view him with the other lights, for a husband should not be either glaringly gloomy, or frigidly frozen.'[8]

At the same time, some travellers were becoming impatient, not only with the excesses of aesthetic sentimentalism inspired by the Claude glass, but with the

The sublime drama of *The Falls of Tivoli* a watercolour by the Swiss artist, Abraham-Louis Ducros, in the Column Room at Stourhead. His work was particularly liked by Richard Colt Hoare, who felt that he painted watercolours like oil paintings.

whole Gilpin-inspired phenomenon of seeing the quest for the picturesque as the ultimate goal of every excursion. By 1793 Edward Clarke confessed that he was tired of the whole thing:

> It has appeared to me that the world is weary of that word *picturesque*, it is forced in upon every occasion; nay, one gentleman, the grand master of landscape, has contrived with the aid of a few muddy sketches, to swell that word to a volume. It is for this reason, that I turn neither to the right nor to the left to visit the mouldering fabrics of my fore-fathers, unless something remains to be said of them besides the *picturesque beauty of their situation.*[9]

'Now, pray, show me anything ancient.'[10] John Byng's earnest request to his guide at Raby Castle epitomises the taste of so many late eighteenth- and early nineteenth-century excursionists, intent on discovering their past. If one had to point to the most distinctive difference between the tastes of tourists in the early 1800s, and those of their predecessors in the early 1700s, it would be this enhanced appreciation of medieval architecture. An awakening historical perspective was coupled with an antiquarianism which, at a popular level, verged on chauvinism, as commentator after commentator urged all true Englishmen to forgo, or at least postpone, their Grand Tour until they were acquainted with their own national heritage. Now, it seemed, tourists were heeding that call:

> Roused, at last, from the lethargy of indifference about what was in their reach, and inspired with more patriotic notions than formerly, of the pleasure and utility of home travels, we have, of late years, seen some of our most enlightened countrymen, as eager to explore the remotest parts of Britain, as they formerly were to cross the Channel, and to pass the Alps.[11]

Two factors – one political, the other aesthetic – gave impetus to this change of emphasis. The uncertainties caused by the aftermath of the French Revolution of 1789, followed by the declaration of war with France in February 1793, disrupted many of Britain's links with Europe. It became extremely difficult for artists and architects to travel to Italy or Greece to study classical remains at first hand, and, indeed, the whole tradition of the Grand Tour was forced to find another focus.

The educated Englishman's enforced isolation led to an acceleration in the growth of interest in native medieval architecture; in churches, abbeys, castles and manor houses; in 'anything ancient', in fact. Tourists were awakened to the aesthetic and emotional impact of a Conway Castle or a Little Moreton Hall, an impact that was heightened by the potential for comparing the present unfavourably with the past, and by the fear that such architecture was fast disappearing: 'I come abroad to view old castles, old manors and old religious houses, before they be quite gone; and that I may compare the ancient structures, and my ideas of their taste, and manners, with the fashions of the present day.'[12]

'Before they be quite gone' – Byng's fears for England's medieval buildings occur over and over again in the literature of the period. *The Topographer* attacked the 'new men, that overrun almost every county in the kingdom, expel the ancient families, destroy the venerable mansions of antiquity, and place in their stead what seemeth good in their own eyes of glaring brick or ponderous stone'.[13] Papers were read to the Society of Antiquaries, describing castles that had recently been demolished, or were in danger of collapsing through neglect. Travellers began to note with regret the damage that encroaching industrialisation was causing to older buildings. And satires on the eighteenth-century conservationist appeared on the London stage – a sure sign that the idea had gained some popular currency:

> DR DRUID: Down with 'em then at once, down with every thing noble and venerable and ancient among you; turn the Tower of London into a Pantheon, make a new Adelphi of the Savoy, and bid adieu to all ages but your own; you will then be no more in the way of deriving dignity from your own progenitors, than you are of transmitting it to your posterity.[14]

Dr Druid, the irascible antiquarian in Cumberland's *The Fashionable Lover*, may have been intended as a figure of fun, with his ravings against the current trend towards the neo-classical. And audiences would certainly have laughed at his want of taste and sensibility. But there were many of his educated contemporaries who would have agreed with him over both the threat to heritage and the moral and social vacuum that would result. Even amongst those who could not accept the extreme position adopted by Dr Druid – and the majority of tourists had, by the beginning of the nineteenth century, been able to steer a middle course between hardline antiquarianism on the one hand, and Celia Fiennes's enthusiasm for the modern on the other – an appreciation of medieval building was just as much a part of their cultural baggage as was their taste for the neo-classical of Adam, or the Palladian splendours of Chiswick. Gothic was fashionable, and polite society reacted accordingly, by going in search of it.

The two examples of Gothic architecture most widely admired during the period were both abbeys, and both highly picturesque – Tintern in the west, and Fountains in the north. The thirteenth-century Cistercian monastery at Tintern was the highlight of a boat trip down the Wye from Ross, a voyage that took in Goodrich and Monmouth Castles before culminating in the sight of this 'perfect skeleton of Gothic architecture', on which 'one might gaze, for hours, with undiminished delight and admiration'.[15] 'All descriptions must fall short of its awful grandeur', wrote one tourist;[16] such responses were commonplace by the 1790s.

But even Tintern paled beside the universal praise that was heaped upon its main rival, Fountains Abbey in Yorkshire. Fountains had been purchased in 1768 by William Aislabie, who saw it as a perfect addition to the elaborate pleasure gardens which his father had begun at Studley Royal forty years before. A journey past rustic bridges and Doric temples, towers and grottos, finally gave way to a

Anthony Walker's engraving, 1758, shows visitors enjoying the Banqueting House and Rotunda at Studley Royal. These two little buildings were erected by John Aislabie c.1730, and are shown here surrounded by formal terraces and clipped hedges. John's son William was to make the garden less formal and more picturesque, moving the Rotunda to the other side of the valley and laying out sweeping lawns.

'view of the finest ruin that it is possible for imagination to conceive'.[17] The majority of travellers seeing Fountains (or indeed, any Gothic ruin) for the first time experienced an essentially emotional response, a feeling of awe at the sight of such decayed magnificence. Nor was this an unconscious reaction – two of the most notable Georgian tour-writers, Arthur Young and William Gilpin, were both moved by the sight of Fountains to speculate on the function of such ruins, and how they should be presented in such a way as to create the proper sensations in the spectator. Young was not interested in style, or the details of the abbey: it was the impression, the emotional impact, that was of primary importance, and he therefore advocated that the fallen masonry and rubble which Aislabie was clearing to make way for turf and artificial paths should be retained. 'Looking as it were stealthily through passages that cannot be passed, heaps of rubbish stopping you

in one place, broken steps preventing both ascent and descent in another; in a word, some parts that cannot be seen at all, others that are half seen, and those fully viewed broken, rugged and terrible' – this was the most effective way to create the right impression. 'In such, the imagination has a free space to range in, and sketches ruins in idea far beyond the boldest strokes of reality.'[18]

In essence, Gilpin agreed with him, lamenting that Aislabie had 'pared away all the bold roughness and freedom of the scene and given every part a trim polish'. However, he went further than Young, suggesting that a monument like Fountains Abbey belonged not to one man, but to the nation:

A legal right the proprietor unquestionably has to deform his ruin as he pleases. But though he fear no King's indictment, he must expect a very

The gardens of Studley Royal, with the ruins of Fountains Abbey in the background, a painting by Balthazar Nebot, c.1760. John Aislabie had tried to buy Fountains Abbey, but fell out with the owner; his son William was more successful and in 1768 was able to incorporate the medieval ruins into his landscape.

severe prosecution in the court of Taste. The refined code of this court does
not consider an elegant ruin as a man's property, on which he may exercise
the irregular sallies of a wanton imagination; but as a deposit of which he is
only the guardian, for the amusement and advantage of posterity. A ruin is
a sacred thing.[19]

This early formulation of the concept of a nation's heritage, of individual buildings
existing somehow in the public domain, may not seem particularly revolutionary
today, when heritage campaigners have established the need for public guardianship of outstanding architecture, and when Listed Buildings Consent is needed
before a private owner can make any alterations to an important piece of architecture. But in Gilpin's day it was an astonishing assertion, which serves here to
indicate the general concern for historic buildings already noted; an awakening
awareness of the way in which the presentation of a site could affect the spectator's
response to it; and the tendency of the polite tourist to look on medieval
monuments as in some sense his or her own property. Fountains Abbey's primary
function was to provide and stimulate aesthetic and emotional satisfaction
amongst those who came to see it, and its owner had a responsibility to ensure
that no action on his part should interfere with that process.

The precise nature of the tourist's response varied dramatically according to the
individual and the site. On one level the appeal was purely visual. In 1794 Uvedale
Price suggested that 'Gothic architecture is generally considered as more
picturesque, though less beautiful than Grecian', and stated that in the windows of
cathedrals and ruined abbeys 'is displayed the triumph of the Picturesque'.[20] But
Price went on to admit that part of the attraction of ruins lay in 'the elegance or
grandeur of their forms – the veneration of high antiquity – or the solemnity of
religious awe'.[21] For many, a primary response to medieval architecture was a feeling of awe at decayed grandeur, a Romantic obsession with the transient nature of
all of man's works. In 1802 Richard Warner, disappointed with the neat gravel
walks and velvet lawns which Aislabie had laid out at Fountains, lamented that
there was 'no one feature to lead to appropriate contemplation, the recollection of
extinguished grandeur, or the conviction of the evanescence of all human labour'.[22]

It was just this sort of self-indulgent frisson that the Georgian visitor
demanded. Touring the south of England in the summer of 1810, Moy Thomas
and Philip Hayman stopped at Netley Abbey in Hampshire, where they sat down
on the grass across from the ivy-clad east window of the ruined church, and
'remained for some minutes indulging that pleasing melancholy musing which is
always excited at the view of such venerable monuments of departed grandeur'.[23]
In accepting the medieval ruin as a stimulus to 'melancholy musing', as a catalyst
which activated certain stock feelings and responses, Thomas, Hayman and their
contemporaries were following in the footsteps of Edmund Burke, who had
defined the experience of the sublime and the beautiful in terms of the emotions
rather than the intellect. They were following Walpole, who had demonstrated
the attractions of Gothic gloom in *The Castle of Otranto*. And they were the spiri-

tual heirs of poets like Thomas Warton, whose *Pleasures of Melancholy* had extolled the joys of ruined abbeys some fifty years before:

> O lead me, Queen Sublime, to solemn glooms
> Congenial with my soul; to cheerless shades,
> To ruin'd seats, to twilight cells and bowers.[24]

But this Romantic association of ideas, whereby a castle or an abbey could evoke a pleasurable sense of loss and regret, was taken further, as a knowledge of the past ceased to be the sole property of the antiquarian and became part of the cultural equipment of the educated tourist. By the beginning of the nineteenth century, the vague musing over man's mortality was supplemented by a more precise reconstruction of the past, as imagination was called on to supply the human element which a Gothic ruin lacked:

> Hail, ye bold turrets, and thou reverend Pile,
> That seem in Age's hoary vest to smile!
> Thou noble Arch, thro' which the massy gate
> Opes to yon Hall in slow and solemn state,
> All-hail! For here creative Fancy reads
> Of ages past, the long-forgotten deeds.[25]

The Topographer's 'creative Fancy' appears in increasing numbers of tourists' accounts of medieval architecture during the last years of the eighteenth century. By the late 1790s, a structure like Tynemouth Priory, perched high on a crag overlooking the sea, had become a peg on which visitors could hang their own highly coloured conception of the past:

> Methinks I see the Abbot . . . hastening from his window towards the verge of this tremendous precipice, and there bidding his beads (good man) for the souls of those unhappy wretches, whom the raging waves are about to swallow; there he stands . . . watching with the utmost care the impending fate of the almost worn out vessel; then offering up tears of supplication for its safety; but alas! 'tis in vain, she sinks and is no more seen, and now he returns comforting himself that what his hands cannot here avail, his prayers may in heaven supply. Imagination must thus supply the past existence of such things, and objects which time hath mouldered into ruin.[26]

When this account of Tynemouth appeared in 1798, the importance of imagination and association in our responses to the external world already had a distinguished pedigree. In the middle of the seventeenth century, Thomas Hobbes had observed that the creative power of the imagination relied on the ability of one image to recall another. John Locke coined the term 'association of ideas' in the fourth edition of his *Essay Concerning Human Understanding* in 1700. Even Burke, who looked for the causes of the sublime and the beautiful in external objects themselves, rather than in the mind, was forced to admit that 'many things affect us after a certain manner, not by any natural powers they have for that purpose, but by association'.[27] With Archibald Alison's *Essays on the Nature and Principles of Taste*, first published in 1790, the importance of association in moulding individual aesthetic judgements was made explicit. Going further than Burke, Alison believed that aesthetic responses come about by the exercise of the imagination:

> The Sublime is increased . . . by whatever tends to increase this exercise of imagination. The field of any celebrated battle becomes sublime from such associations. No man, acquainted with English history, could behold the field of Agincourt, without some emotion of this kind. The additional conceptions which this association produces, and which fill the mind of the spectator on the prospect of that memorable field, diffuse themselves in some measure over the scene, and give it a sublimity which does not naturally belong to it.[28]

Alison goes on to suggest that the antiquarian's pleasure in 'the relics of former ages' stems from their power to evoke other images: 'The dress, the furniture, the arms of the times, are so many assistances to his imagination, in guiding or directing its exercise, and, offering him a thousand sources of imagery, provide him with an almost inexhaustible field in which his memory and his fancy may expatiate.'[29]

In this new climate, Elizabethan houses were being revalued and slowly rehabilitated. We have seen how Horace Walpole reacted to Hardwick – 'vast rooms, no taste'. But within thirty years his judgements had been rejected by the majority who, in line with their espousal of creative fancy as a means of interpreting a country house, had come to see in Tudor buildings an image of Merry England and old English hospitality. William Bray, writing of the early sixteenth-century Compton Wynyates in Warwickshire, noted: '[W]hen this house was built it is plain that the owner could not have a single idea of the beauty arising from prospects . . . But it stood in the centre of a noble estate, and was sufficient for the purposes of hospitality, which did more real honour to the possessor than the most elegant modern seat, where it is wanting.'[30] Older houses were acquiring the moral connotations of a better, less effete lifestyle that outweighed their aesthetic shortcomings. As evidence of a vanished way of life, they had a message for the tourist, an historical value which took pride of place over their architectural merits.

This change in attitude towards the architecture of the past is exemplified in the new response to Hardwick Hall. Not only was it thought (quite wrongly, in fact) to be a perfect specimen of untouched late Elizabethan work, but Hardwick possessed the added attraction for the Romantic tourist of having been one of the prisons of Mary, Queen of Scots, even though the house had not been begun till two or three years after her execution. The Gothic novelist Ann Radcliffe gave free rein to her imagination during a visit there in 1796:

> We followed, not without emotion, the walk, which Mary had so often trodden . . . The scene of Mary's arrival and her feelings upon entering this

solemn shade came unvoluntarily to the mind; the noise of horses' feet and many voices from the court; her proud yet gentle and melancholy look, as, led by my Lord Keeper, she passed slowly up the hall; his somewhat obsequious, yet jealous and vigilant air, while, awed by her dignity and beauty, he remembers the terrors of his own Queen; the silence and anxiety of her maids, and the bustle of the surrounding attendants.[31]

The two Halls at Hardwick came into their own again with the search for the Picturesque. This romantic view of the ruins of the Old Hall was sketched by William Hunt in 1828.

The rage to construct images of the past, no matter how unstable the basis for such images, was not confined to the Georgian. As a means of structuring and interpreting one's experience of architecture, imaginative reconstruction was to become a cliché. It survived well into the twentieth century, and has recently achieved a new respectability, as research into the social history of the country house has encouraged a more scholarly approach among visitors. But in the nineteenth century, the concept of Romantic association, the notion of responding to architecture and art not on its own terms, but by reference to something outside itself, was to grow beyond imaginary figures from the past like the Abbot of Tynemouth Priory, beyond historical personalities such as the doomed Mary Queen of Scots, to take in the enormous impact of literature on the popular imagination. Scenes from great novels, and visits to 'the homes and haunts of the most eminent British poets', to quote the title of an early Victorian guide to the subject, played an important part in moulding the perceptions of the tourist.

Of course this is hardly surprising when one considers the rising literacy rate
during the 1800s, especially among an expanding urban middle class which was
beginning to see country-house visiting as a legitimate leisure pursuit. At
Penshurst Place in Kent, where three times a week a coach would take the tourist
from London to the gates of the house in about three hours, one could stroll
through the grounds and imagine 'Waller and Saccharissa bandying compliments
beneath the noble beeches, now called Saccharissa's Walk', or even conjure up 'Sir

MARIA
D G
SCOTIÆ
PIISSIMA REGINA
FRANCIÆ DOWERIA
ANNO
ÆTATIS REGNI
36
ANGLICÆ CAPTIVA
10
S H
1578

Left: Mary Queen of Scots, a portrait probably by Rowland Lockey, in the Long Gallery at Hardwick. The Earl of Shrewsbury, Bess of Hardwick's fourth husband, had custody of the Queen during her long captivity in England.

Although Mary Queen of Scots was executed before Bess of Hardwick built her New Hall, eighteenth-century romantic imagination linked the two together. The Dukes of Devonshire obliged by taking the carved panel of the Queen's arms from their house at Chatsworth and installing it in a room furnished in the Elizabethan style that became known as the Mary Queen of Scots Room (*far left*).

Right: Charlecote Park: a view of the east front through the Elizabethan gatehouse, with Sir Thomas Lucy's arms shown over the arch.

Far right: An early Victorian reconstruction of the famous poaching scene, with the young William Shakespeare, caught redhanded by the gamekeeper, brought before Sir Thomas Lucy in front of the gatehouse of his Tudor mansion at Charlecote. This romantic image comes from Nash's *The Mansions of England*, 1839–42.

Philip [Sidney] pacing the broad terrace of the garden, with his admired sister Pembroke, and Edmund Spenser, deep in dreams of chivalry and poetry, which no sound of steam-engines, nor bruit of reform and registrations, nor arrival of morning paper, in those days disturbed.'[32] Or the tourist could visit Charlecote in Warwickshire, to see the birthplace of the legend of the young Shakespeare poaching deer in the park, and being brought before the owner, Sir Thomas Lucy, for punishment:

Let us not disturb the story which tallies with likelihood as well as tradition. If we cease to believe that Shakespeare chased the deer over the Charlecote sward, – that he stood a prisoner in this hall, with no friend at his back, and little in his purse, we obliterate a red letter day in literary annals . . .; we do more, we rob this mansion of its living interest, this hall of the literary halo which centuries have sanctioned; we disenchant those parks and ponds, limes and elms, osiers and oaks of the charm which draws the world to walk among them.[33]

This interest in literary associations was a manifestation of the Romantic conception of the artist as hero, a by-product of which was the growth of the cult of the personality; and the Romantics certainly had an enormous influence on the tourists' appreciation of their environment. William Wordsworth's impact on the Lake District as a centre for excursions and holidays (his own *Guide Through the Lakes* appeared in 1835) focused on the natural landscape, but two other Romantics, Lord Byron and Sir Walter Scott, have a place in the history of architectural taste.

Byron's influence is less pervasive than that of Scott, and relates more to one particular property than to a general way of seeing buildings, although the young Fanny Symonds, on holiday in Cornwall in 1836, definitely seems to have absorbed some Byronic attitudes: standing at Land's End, she found that the 'shriek of the Cormorants [and] the plaintive cry of the other sea fowl rendered the spot melancholy and romantic. I remained there some time; you forget the world and feel *indeed alone*.'[34] But the poet's most significant effect on country-house visiting concerns his family home, Newstead Abbey in Nottinghamshire, which in the years following his death at Missolonghi in 1824, became a place of pilgrimage for a huge number of tourists.

To a public steeped in the Romantic imagination, and reared on a diet of *Childe Harold's Pilgrimage* and *Don Juan*, Newstead must have seemed almost too good to be true. Like Lord Henry and Lady Amundeville's 'Gothic Babel of a thousand years' in *Don Juan*, the Abbey was 'An old, old monastery once, and now/Still older mansion, of a rich and rare/Mix'd Gothic':

> Huge halls, long galleries, spacious chambers, join'd
> By no quite lawful marriage of the arts,
> Might shock a connoisseur; but, when combined,
> Form'd a whole which, irregular in parts,
> Yet left a grand impression on the mind,
> At least of those whose eyes are in their hearts.[35]

And with the fashionable emphasis on an emotional response to architecture, visitors to Newstead most certainly did have their eyes in their hearts. The converted Augustinian priory, complete with crypt, cloisters and ruined church, was a perfect setting in which to absorb the atmosphere of the past. Although Byron had sold his family home in 1816, late Georgian or Victorian tourists could see the 'glorious remnant of the Gothic pile/(While yet the church was Rome's)' which 'stood half apart';[36] they could explore the poet's bedroom, 'an object of interest to all visitors, more especially as it is said to be still kept in the same state as when occupied by his lordship'. Next door, they were shown the Haunted Chamber, 'a dismal room, where, as it is commonly said by the guide, the spirit of a restless monk (probably he whose skull the poet converted into a drinking-cup) still occasionally intrudes his ghostly presence'[37] – perhaps the very same monk seen by Don Juan, 'array'd/In cowl and beads, and dusky garb', who 'moved as shadowy as the sisters weird,/But slowly; and as he passed Juan by/Glanced, without pausing, on him a bright eye.'[38] And he could walk the cloisters, as Byron had done, and read in his guidebook that 'there are still tenants to be found beneath the pavement', although – and this a rather wistful note, one feels – 'there are no sepulchral slabs'.[39]

Newstead Abbey represents a coming together of two important motifs in nineteenth-century country-house visiting. It acted as a focus for the contemporary concern with medieval architecture as a stimulus to individual and deeply felt emotions – Gothic as a mode of vision rather than simply a style of building; and, for a public that was devouring literature in increasing quantities, it had strong associations with leading members of the literary movement which had done so much to popularise such attitudes. If art mirrored life, then, at Newstead, life was in turn mirroring art in a striking fashion, and if the tourist could obtain a vicarious thrill from recalling just how mad, bad and dangerous to know Byron was, or could complacently ask: 'Time, will thy progress distort the poet's fame, and when the impression of the brilliant sparklings of his genius are somewhat faded, will the misanthrope, the libertine, and the voluntary maniac be alone remembered?'[40] – then so much the better.

It is perhaps worth recalling just how popular Byron was with the general public. The first two cantos of *Childe Harold* went through seven editions in a month, and had sold 4,500 copies within six months of its appearance in 1812. The later poems did even better: writing about *The Corsair*, Byron's publisher, Murray, said that he sold 'on the day of publication – a thing perfectly unprecedented – ten thousand copies'.[41] But even these sales figures pale in comparison with those of the most popular Romantic, Sir Walter Scott. Scott's *Lay of the Last Minstrel* (1805) went through fourteen editions, and sold 33,000 copies, in its first twenty years; *Marmion* and *The Lady of the Lake* were at least as successful. Of the novels, *Rob Roy* (1817) sold 10,000 in three weeks; 7,000 copies of *The Fortunes of Nigel* sold in London by 10.30 on the morning of publication in 1822; and 35,000 copies of the 1829 collected edition of the Waverley novels were sold each month.

Scott's home, Abbotsford in Roxburghshire, and his burial-place at nearby Dryburgh Abbey, became places of pilgrimage, much as Newstead Abbey was:

> The hall-door is opened – and here breathed, and for a while lived, the greatest of intellectual mortals in this country, after Shakespeare, Bacon, Milton, and Newton. You walk into Sir Walter's study, sit in his chair, gaze

The Lake District has been exciting the artistic imagination for two centuries. Coleridge described the Lodore Falls on the shores of Derwentwater as 'beyond all rivalry the first and best thing in the whole Lake Country'. Francis Towne was one of many painters who tried to capture its wild beauty – this picture (*right*) was painted in 1786. It is still possible to lose oneself in that wild beauty today (*far right*) – a remarkable feat considering that sixteen million tourists flock to the Lakes every year.

upon the motley furniture; and hard by, in a boudoir, behold his straw hat, jacket, waistcoat, trousers, high shoes, and walking-stick – in all which he was wont to be arrayed – hanging upon a couple of nails. You cannot fail to be sensibly affected.[42]

But, more importantly, the places described in the novels and poems were seen as literary rather than architectural creations. 'AW', on an excursion to the Midlands and the north-west of England in 1832 (only one week before Scott's death on 21

September), constantly commented on various architectural sites mentioned in the artist's books: 'We had a fine view from the Windgates of the ruins of Peveril Castle [in Derbyshire], celebrated by Sir Walter Scott'; at Castletown on the Isle of Man 'there is little worth notice, save Rushen Castle celebrated in Sir Walter Scott's novel of *Peveril of the Peak*'; and at Peel, 'here also is a castle, in ruins situated on a rock, containing an old Cathedral with many tombs and vaults among which the spectre of a dog is said to walk at stated hours, which Sir WS has mentioned in one of his notes in his *Lay of the Last Minstrel*'.[43]

It was quite natural for the tourist to use Scott's work as a point of reference. The artist's strong sense of place, his method of weaving historical romances around identifiable sites, and his gift for picturesque description, were all calculated to appeal to the excursionist's ideas of creative fancy, providing a ready-made form of imaginative reconstruction, and bringing a property to life, even if that 'life' operated on a purely literary level. The consequences for the various houses, castles and abbeys which figure in Scott's works – Kenilworth, Warwick, Woodstock – were that they became firmly established points on nineteenth-century tourist routes. In the eyes of some commentators, the novelist had virtually created the Scottish tourist industry:

> See what he has done for Scotland. See every summer, and all summer long, what thousands pour into that beautiful country, exploring every valley, climbing every mountain, sailing on every firth and loch, and spreading themselves and their money all through the land. And what roads and steam-vessels, what cars and coaches, are prepared for them! what inns are erected![44]

Back in England, Ashby de la Zouch, with its castle, large new hotel and baths, became, for a while, a fashionable spa town, partly as a result of interest in *Ivanhoe*. The visitor could recall Scott's romantic vision of highly coloured pageantry and chivalry in a largely mythical past:

> Gradually the galleries became filled with knights and nobles, in their robes of peace, whose long and rich-tinted mantles were contrasted with the gayer and more splendid habits of the ladies ... The lower and interior space was soon filled by substantial yeomen and burghers, and such of the lesser gentry as, from modesty, poverty, or dubious title, durst not assume any higher place.[45]

The myth of Merry England, with its strictly ordered society and its chivalric code of values, appealed more and more strongly to the upper strata of a society that was in a state of flux and felt under threat from social and political unrest at home and abroad. The French Revolution was recent enough to provide an awful example of what might happen if the upper classes lost control; while Peterloo and demonstrations against the Six Acts in 1819 were a reminder that it *could* happen here.

So perhaps, on one level at least, the tourist's response to English architecture was tinged with a sort of regret, a yearning for a past age which was at once more colourful and more secure. Creative fancy thus became not only a means of structuring and interpreting one's experience of a house, or a castle, or an abbey. It became an escape route into a safer, more congenial world.

Little Moreton Hall in Cheshire, built in the fifteenth and sixteenth centuries by the prosperous Moretons, gentlemen farmers. By the nineteenth century it was the home of a considerably less prosperous farmer and his animals, but represented a highly attractive romantic vision for the painter J. S. Cotman. This engraving by Thomas Tagg/John Smith after Cotman appeared in *The Architectural Antiquities of Great Britain* published in 1835.

CHAPTER 6

A Well-Pleased Throng of People

ON THE NIGHT of Saturday, 30 October 1841, the Tower of London was devastated by fire. The Armoury was particularly badly damaged, and many of its contents were destroyed. Following a month-long clearing-up operation, the Tower was partially re-opened to the public on Monday, 6 December, to allow visitors to see the extent of the destruction, even though restoration was still far from complete. It was a commercial venture: a mandatory charge of sixpence a head was made at the 'Armoury ticket-office' at the main entrance. According to *The Times*:

> The ruins of the Armoury, consisting of musket-barrels, locks, bayonets, &c, have been piled up in several places, as have also been many of the trophies taken at Waterloo, and at other military and naval engagements. The whole are enclosed with small wooden railings; but the view to visitors is unobstructed. The purchasers of tickets are also admitted to the centre of the Grand Storehouse (attended by the warders, in the same way as in the Armouries), whence an excellent view of the whole of the ruins is obtained.[1]

Quite apart from the novelty of presenting a major disaster as a tourist attraction – and charging for it on a fixed-price basis – the authorities were obviously intent on capitalising on the situation as much as possible. A souvenir shop, in the shape of two marquees, was set up under the auspices of the Board of Ordnance between the Bowyer Tower and the Brick Tower: 'various specimens saved from the ruins, showing the effects of fire on the different metals, and other substances destroyed by it, are exposed for sale to visitors at fixed prices.'[2]

Reactions to this commercial approach were mixed. Attendances at the Tower during the first week, when the site was open from Monday to Saturday, totalled 2,341. The initial response was poor, with only 156 visitors turning up on the first day, but this was put down to the bad weather, since on Tuesday, which was sunny, the figure almost quadrupled. (*The Times* noted that most of the tourists were women, and that the majority 'purchased some relics of the late disastrous conflagration'.[3]) The week after Christmas, 2,494 tourists bought tickets to view the scenes of destruction, but within a couple of months, attendances had dropped off considerably, with only 543 in the last week of February.

The destruction of the small armoury at the Tower of London on the night of 30 October 1841, from an engraving by C. Hullmandel after William Smith.

In contrast to the Board of Ordnance's attitude towards the public as a potential source of revenue at the Tower, the authorities had taken a radically different approach to the opening of another palace, Hampton Court, three years earlier.

A Yeoman Warder taking visitors around the Great Horse Armoury in 1841, just before the fire that devastated the Tower of London.

Like other major buildings, Hampton Court had, of course, been open to certain sections of the public for hundreds of years. By the early nineteenth century the operation had been formalised to some extent, and some of the state apartments were being shown on payment of one shilling or more. Contemporary accounts suggest that the shilling charge was less than good value. One visitor in 1823 remarked:

> These princely halls have come to be almost as silent as their master's tomb.
> They have nothing to echo back but the hurried footstep of a single domestic … or the unintelligible jargon of a superannuated dependant, as he

describes to a few straggling visitors (without looking at either) the objects of art that have been deposited in them, like treasures in a tomb.[4]

With the death in April 1838 of Hampton Court's Housekeeper, Lady Emily Montague, who had received an income from the admission charges to the palace, Queen Victoria, who had succeeded to the throne the previous year, abolished the office of Housekeeper, and it was decided that certain parts of the house should be thrown open to the public free of charge. As a result, Hampton Court was closed on 15 August 1838, to allow the necessary arrangements to be made. It formally opened its doors to the masses three months later.

Nothing like this had ever happened before, and not surprisingly, such a radical move provoked strong opposition and dire warnings of vandalism, drunkenness and violent behaviour. It was certainly true that the number of visitors increased dramatically: admissions rose from only a few hundred a year in the 1830s to 115,971 in 1839 and 122,339 in 1840. The average for the two decades between 1850 and 1870 was around 200,000, with peaks of 350,848 in 1851 and 369,162 in 1862 (the two Exhibition years).[5]

As to the extent of the damage and bad behaviour, the opinions of observers varied considerably. One of the most positive was the reformer William Howitt, writing in 1840. In his *Visits to Remarkable Places*, he made it clear that he saw in the liberalised access arrangements at Hampton Court a sort of natural justice:

> [The palace] is, as it should be, given up to the use and refreshment of the people. It is the first step towards the national appropriation of public property. It is long since it was said, 'The king has got his own again,' and it is now fitting that the people should have their own again. Of all the palaces, the towers, the abbeys, and cathedrals, which have been raised with the wealth and ostensibly for the benefit of the people, none till lately have been freely open to the footsteps of the multitude. They have been jealously retained for the enjoyment of an exclusive few, or have been made engines to extort still further payment from those out of whose pockets they were raised. But ... now this charming old palace of Hampton Court has been made the daily resort of any, and of all, of the English people who choose to tread the pavements, and disport themselves in the gardens, and gaze on the works of art, which for ages were wont only to be accessible to the royal, the aristocratic, and the ecclesiastical dignitary and their retainers.[6]

In Howitt's suggestion that Hampton Court was in some sense 'public property', one can see an extension of Gilpin's remarks on Fountains Abbey, his warning that the proprietor was 'only the guardian, for the amusement and advantage of posterity'.[7] But Gilpin, writing at the end of the eighteenth century, had only advised Aislabie to 'expect a very severe prosecution in the court of Taste' if he tampered with Fountains; his notion of 'posterity' involved a collective elite of cognoscenti and would-be cognoscenti, and the idea that the nation's architectural and artistic

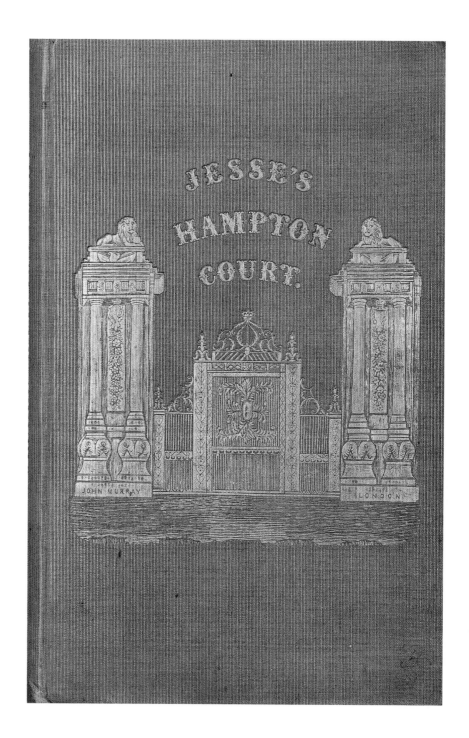

JESSE'S
HAMPTON
COURT.

JOHN MURRAY   LONDON

heritage belonged to the mass of the people would have been as unthinkable to him as universal suffrage.

Howitt, on the other hand, was clearly taking the concept of a national heritage considerably further. One of his most virulent critics was the anonymous reviewer of *Visits to Remarkable Places* in *The Gentleman's Magazine* of May 1840:

> We grant that some people want to make [palaces and cathedrals] public property, not for the sake of more freely participating in their services, but of getting possession of their revenues. The Reform Bill has done one thing: it has dragged out to light all the mean, base, sordid desires of the selfish; as well as given encouragement to the busy, meddling, swaggering, vulgar insolence of the low-born bully; the former of whom grudges the sovereign what the meanest individual has, an undisturbed home; and the latter is not content unless he can, at will, imprint his hoofs upon its polished floors.[8]

As far as *The Gentleman's Magazine* was concerned, free access to Hampton Court had proved an unmitigated disaster. The reviewer reported that flowers were constantly being stolen from the gardens; police in attendance in the state apartments had to be always on their guard, since 'instances of conduct have occurred that we should not expect to have heard of, and which we could not name with propriety but by borrowing the foreign word of "*immondezza*"'; and 'handicrafts men in leathern aprons ... have not ceased to be the most intolerable nuisance that any town was infested with, and which has made Hampton Court a place where ladies cannot walk out unprotected'.[9]

Howitt's experience was rather different. Except for some scratches on the panelling of the Great Staircase, which had apparently appeared before the palace was opened free of charge, he could not 'learn that the slightest exhibition of what has been considered the English love of demolition, has been made. Never have I seen, at all times that I have been there, a more orderly or more well-pleased throng of people.'[10]

The debate over the behaviour of working-class visitors eventually died down, only to resurface twelve years later in the columns of *The Times*, when an anonymous correspondent complained of a speech made by the Sabbatarian Daniel Wilson. Wilson had attacked the practice of opening Hampton Court on Sunday afternoons, and quoted a friend as saying that the place was 'a hell upon earth. The people come intoxicated, and the scenes in these gardens on the afternoon of the Lord's Day are beyond description.'[11] The correspondent strongly refuted Wilson's charge – 'I, Sir, distinctly declare it to be false' – and three days later W. C. Celle, organist at Hampton Court Chapel, wrote in support: 'Sir – Having attended every Sunday for the last seven years at Hampton-court Palace, I have had every opportunity of seeing the conduct of the thousands who attend there. I therefore consider myself bound to say the conduct of the "masses" is orderly, quiet, and respectful, nor do I ever remember seeing a drunken character.'[12]

Hampton Court Palace was opened to the public in 1840, and this was one of the first guidebooks produced. *Jesse's Hampton Court* was published by John Murray, specialists in travel books.

Finally, after a gap of a fortnight, the Revd Wilson himself replied in defence of his original comments:

> The crowd of visitors at the Palace on the Sunday afternoons, during the last summer, has been enormous; their conduct in many cases was most offensive; many arrived in a state of intoxication. The pictures were in danger of serious injury from drunken persons who passed through the rooms. All the servants are sworn in as constables; they are not infrequently exposed to abuse of the grossest character. There is a marked difference between the respectability and good conduct of those who visit the Palace on the week-days and those of the Sunday assemblage.[13]

Wilson's differentiation between week-day visitors and Sunday visitors involves more than a simple distinction between the god-fearing and the godless: implicit in his remarks is the notion that the working classes – who would, of course, find it difficult to come to the palace on a week-day – did not deserve to participate in the national heritage, and were ill-equipped to benefit from an experience of it. Their rowdiness would inevitably spoil it for everybody else.

The opposite view, perhaps more typical of the age in its message of improvement and self-help, was proposed by Howitt, a little later in his essay on Hampton Court. Commenting on the crowds of day-trippers walking through the state apartments 'intent on the works of Raphael, Titian, Correggio, Lely, Vandyke, Kneller, Rembrandt, Rubens', Howitt suggested:

> Here surely was significant indication of a change in the popular mind in the course of one generation, which must furnish an answer to those who ask what has education done for the masses, and most pregnant with matter of buoyant augury for the future. Those who do not see in such a spectacle that the march of intellect, and the walking abroad of the schoolmaster, are something more than things to furnish a joke or a witticism, are blind indeed to the signs of the times, and to the certainty that the speed of sound knowledge amongst the people will yet make this nation more deserving of the epithet of a nation of princes.[14]

Popular responses to Hampton Court probably lay somewhere between these two poles, as can be seen from 'Bill Banks's Day Out', an 1868 short story by Thomas Wright, who wrote under the pseudonym of 'The Journeyman Engineer'. Although the piece is fiction, it has a ring of truth to it, both in its practical details and in its approach to working-class attitudes to art and architecture. The narrator, a London stoker, and his wife, have taken two places on an organised excursion to the Palace, in company with some friends. The visit follows an established pattern: the owner of the van in which the party travels has contracted to provide a good dinner, at half a crown a head. It will be ready at three o'clock, and when Bill and his wife and friends arrive at Hampton Court at eleven, they are shown the 'quiet spot near the Wilderness', where they must meet to take their meal.

The superb wrought iron gates, flanked by lions, that were one of the popular points of entry into Hampton Court. This watercolour by David Cox Junior shows tourists getting ready for their visit, c.1840.

They spend the next three or four hours exploring the Palace:

> We went through the different rooms, a-looking at the pictures and painted
> ceilings, and all that, and very nice they was, though we couldn't quite
> understand some of 'em, 'specially the ceilings, which were all gods and
> goddesses, and cupids, and them sort of people as you read about in old
> poetry-books, and see in the statues at the Crystal Palace, and as I don't
> believe ever was in reality. However, we couldn't stay to look at 'em very
> particular, as it took us all our time looking pretty sharp to get through all
> the rooms by dinner-time.[15]

The dinner – beef, mutton, ham, fruit tarts, bottled ale and a small cask of porter –

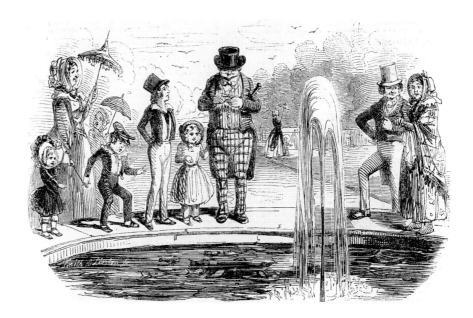

A holiday group at Hampton Court, from the *Illustrated London News*, 10 June 1843. 'Now this charming old palace . . . has been made the daily resort of any, and of all, of the English people who choose to tread the pavements, and disport themselves in the gardens.'

is 'a first-rater', and afterwards everybody strolls through the grounds until five o'clock, when the party returns to London and the Alhambra for an evening's entertainment to round off the day.

Bill Banks's day out is primarily a social occasion, an opportunity to take a break from work in the company of friends. His reaction to the contents of the house is one of interest rather than educated involvement, and discussion of the works of art centres on the disparity between the aesthetic and moral qualities of Lely's Court Beauties:

> 'Well, I never saw such a lot of fine pictures together before, as what's here.'
> 'Well, there's some beautiful ones among them, that's certain,' said a young fellow as was out for the day with his intended, ''specially some of the likenesses of ladies; it does a fellow's eyes good to look at 'em.'
> 'Ay,' I says, 'some of 'em were court beauties in their day, and I daresay gave many a fine swell the heartache.'
> 'Well, if all's true as is said about them, some of them weren't no better than they should have been,' says Polly Edwards, quite sharplike . . .
> 'No, that they weren't,' says an old woman with spectacles on, and a face that sour-looking that it's a wonder to me it hadn't turned the porter . . .
> 'They were a pack of trolloping madams as ought to have been ashamed of themselves; that's what they were.'[16]

The opening up of Hampton Court was a milestone in the developing relationship between the owner of a property and the public, for two reasons. True, the owner was in this case the Crown, and the property a royal palace, but, even so, the introduction of free access to a house of such importance, within easy reach of a massive urban population, could be said to have inaugurated a new era of popular tourism, marking the beginning of a slow but steady move away from the elaborate system of social controls which had operated to exclude most people from the country house ever since the breakdown of 'good lordship' in the late sixteenth century.

The second reason for Hampton Court's importance is that it served as a battle-ground over which conservatives and progressives could fight for their respective views on the relationship between 'the masses' and culture, each coming up with different answers to the question, 'What is the point of letting Bill Banks experience our architectural and artistic heritage?' The battle was also going on elsewhere, of course: wherever a free library, or a new museum, or a public art gallery, was proposed, its value as an educational tool and civilising influence on the lower classes would be debated.

This question was itself part of a wider debate on the condition of England, which was prompted during the 1830s and 1840s by concern for issues of public health and public order. Traditional working-class recreations were denigrated and suppressed: 'The very essence of our laws has been against the social meetings of the humble, which have been called idleness, and against the amusements of the poor, which have been stigmatised as disorder.'[17]

And, inevitably, if drinking, brawling and the pleasures of the flesh – all of which were regarded as typical proletarian entertainments – were to be done away with, there would arise the need for something to replace those recreations, something which would improve the minds of the masses, and which would also serve as a means of social control:

> There must be safety valves for the mind; that is, there must be means for its pleasurable, profitable and healthful exertion. These means it is in our power to render safe and innocent: these means in too many instances have been rendered dangerous and guilty . . . [It is] the great but neglected truth, that moral education, in spite of all the labours of direct instructors, is really acquired in hours of recreation.[18]

Rational recreation, in which the working man's mind was improved on both a cultural and a moral level, was seen as the answer, and the call grew for the provision of open spaces – open-air sitting-rooms for the poor, as Octavia Hill was later to call them – public art galleries and museums, and cheap or free circulating libraries. As early as 1834, a parliamentary select committee on drunkenness was recommending, as an antidote to the evils of alcohol:

> the establishment . . . of public walks, and gardens, or open spaces for healthy and athletic exercises in the open air, in the immediate vicinity of every town, of an extent and character adapted to its population; and of district and parish libraries, museums and reading rooms, accessible at the

The Great Vine, Hampton Court Palace.
It has generally from 2000 to 3000 bunches of grapes upon it, and is 110 feet long.

28,

Two of the popular attractions at Hampton Court were turned into postcards.
Above: The Great Vine, a Black Hamburg of considerable age, which could be viewed from a special corridor in the Vinehouse.
Below: Visitors in the Maze – an experience immortalised by Jerome K. Jerome in *Three Men in a Boat*.

The Maze, Hampton Court Palace

lowest rate of charge; so as to admit of one or the other being visited in any weather, and at any time.[19]

This early emphasis on open spaces in particular, harks back to the Romantic notion of close contact with nature as a good in itself, and looks forward to a time at the end of the century when the country house and its estate would come to symbolise a lost rural paradise, a set of organic natural values representing all that was best about England, in sharp contrast to the urbanised, industrialised reality. But at the time, laissez-faire political theories led to a general reluctance to implement such proposals, and, in any case, they had, initially at least, little impact on the country-house visiting public. They arose out of a humanitarian concern for the moral and physical welfare of a new industrial working class, living – often in appalling conditions – in rapidly expanding towns and cities; a concern that often went hand in hand with a fear of social disorder and political unrest.

The problem was thus essentially urban, and since the masses were unlikely to be able to make extended journeys into the countryside, where of course most country houses were situated, the solution involved the provision of rational recreation in or near large centres of population. The venue in Hyde Park of the Great Exhibition of 1851 made it readily accessible to Londoners – the Crystal Palace drew more than six million visitors during the 144 days it was open – although even here, occasional 'high-priced days' helped to ensure social segregation.

Aristocratic owners were called upon to play their part. Art and architecture were acknowledged as improving and civilising influences, and the landowner was obliged by his position to extend the privilege of experiencing them beyond the traditional circle of upper-middle-class excursionists. George Gilbert Scott defined the role of the Victorian landowner in his *Secular and Domestic Architecture*, published in 1857:

> Wealth must always bring its responsibilities, but a landed proprietor is especially in a responsible position. He is the natural head of his parish or district – in which he should be looked up to as the bond of union between the classes. To him the poor man should look up for protection; those in doubt or difficulty for advice; the ill disposed for reproof or punishment; the deserving, of all classes, for consideration and hospitality; and all for a dignified, honourable and Christian example.[20]

During the early years of Victoria's reign, there was, in fact, little increase in the demand to view country houses. But with the rapid development of a network of railways, more and more tourists took the opportunity to move out of town for a few days, or even for a day-trip; and, as branch lines came to connect the homes of the aristocracy with large towns and cities, those homes became natural targets for the excursionist.

In the early days, a journey by railway was as much of an attraction for the tourist as was the destination. Writing of a tour taken in September 1832, an

Queen Victoria opening the Great
Exhibition at the Crystal Palace in
Hyde Park, London, on 1 May 1851.
More than six million visitors
attended in five months, with a peak
of 109,760 on 8 October, three days
before it was to close.

anonymous diarist was clearly as excited by a train ride on the Manchester to
Liverpool line as he was by his visits to Chatsworth, Peveril Castle and Eaton
Hall:

> The pleasure of travelling by the rail road is hardly to be described, the
> safety, the velocity, and the ease (for you may fancy you are sitting in a room)
> is delightful. A short distance from Liverpool, the locomotive engine is
> taken off and a rope is attached to the train, which is affixed to a stationary
> engine. And in this way you enter a tunnel about half a mile long, when you
> come into a court-yard, filled with omnibuses, chaises & cars to take the
> passengers and baggage to the different hotels. There is also another tunnel,
> close to the one I have mentioned, for goods, which extends one and a
> half miles, cut through solid lime stone rock, and lit up with gas, down to
> the docks, through which the trains of carriages and goods quite roar like
> thunder.[21]

This element of entertainment was maintained and exploited by the London and
Greenwich Railway, which opened in 1836. The managing director of the L&GR
was accompanied in his journeys along the line by an official bugler, who played
'See the Conquering Hero Comes', and objects of interest, including a 'wonderful
naval torpedo, invented by the Earl of Dundonald', were exhibited at stations
along the route.[22] But as an awareness of the commercial potential of the railway
grew, developers were quick to cash in on the new means of transport. In 1840 299
Acts were passed relating to railways, sanctioning the construction of some 3,000
miles of track. Although many of these projects were subsequently abandoned, by
1860 nearly 10,500 miles of line had been laid, a figure which had virtually doubled
by the early 1890s.

While this huge expansion helped to democratise tourism, many lower-middle-
class and working-class families could not avail themselves of the opportunities
because of their lack of free time. It was not until the mid-1860s that legislation
and trade-union activity brought reductions in working hours and the introduction of a Saturday half-holiday in a number of trades, while railwaymen on the
Great Northern seem to have been the first manual workers to receive regular paid
holidays, in 1872 (although in the late 1860s bank clerks in the City could expect up
to three weeks off after a certain length of service.) Thereafter it was possible for
visits to the seaside and the country to be taken by working people.

Some twenty years earlier, Charles Knight, publisher, author of *Knowledge is
Power* and leading light of the Society for the Diffusion of Useful Knowledge,
advocated the recreational benefits of the railway:

> The EXCURSION TRAIN is one of our best public instructors. It is also one
> of the cheapest. At a rate for second and third-class passengers, varying
> from twenty miles to fifty-five miles for a shilling, or from a little above a
> halfpenny to less than a farthing a mile, hundreds of thousands of travellers

from London, during 1850, have been carried into the heart of our most beautiful inland Scenery ... Nor is this all. From all the great manufacturing and commercial towns, Excursion Trains are constantly bearing the active and intelligent artisans, with their families, to some interesting locality, for a happy and rational holiday. The amount of pleasure and information thus derived, and of prejudice thus removed, cannot be estimated at too high a rate.[23]

This notion of broadening one's mind by making excursions by rail led to an increased demand for access to the nation's country houses, and as the eighteenth-century practice of making an extended summer tour by chaise or on horseback dwindled, it was replaced by the organised outing to a specific property or group of properties – the day-trip, in other words.

The formal systems of controlling admission which had grown up in the eighteenth century as a reaction to demands for access from polite society continued to spread during the nineteenth. By the middle of the century, entry by ticket was becoming increasingly common. Following the successful experiment at Hampton Court, entry to the State Apartments at Windsor was free by the 1850s, but it was by ticket only, obtainable from Messrs Colnaghi, 14 Pall Mall East; Wright, 60 Pall Mall; Ackermann, 96 The Strand; Mitchell, 33 Old Bond Street; and Moon, 20 Threadneedle Street. Tickets were valid for up to one week from the date of issue, and official guidebooks were also available at the same places, priced at one penny each.

One wonders if Messrs Colnaghi, Wright, Ackermann, Mitchell and Moon operated any discreet vetting procedures. It seems clear from a mid-Victorian guide to Newstead Abbey that its owner, W. F. Webb, certainly did:

> The proprietor is most generous in granting permission to view the Abbey, under certain restrictions which every right thinking person will consider absolutely necessary. It being a family residence, in a private domain, cannot be thrown open for persons to visit, indiscriminately, from mere idle curiosity.
>
> Parties desirous of seeing the Abbey, for its associations or other commendable reasons, must a few days previous, write the proprietor for permission; all such applications being courteously responded to.[24]

Implicit in this statement is a slight feeling of being threatened: visiting a house for 'its associations or other commendable reasons' is, one feels, what distinguishes the Victorian equivalent of the polite tourist from the less welcome sightseer and his 'mere idle curiosity'. The fact that Webb felt it necessary to issue such a warning gives some indication of the social changes which were taking place in what was becoming an embryonic tourist industry.

The organised excursion was perhaps the most distinctive feature of country-house visiting during the second half of the nineteenth century. Tourist societies sprang up all over the country:

An admission ticket produced in 1823 by the auctioneer Harry Phillips for entry to the view-and-sale at William Beckford's extraordinary house, Fonthill Abbey in Wiltshire.

FONTHILL ABBEY 1823

THIS TICKET WILL ADMIT TWO VISITORS ON ANY TWO DAYS DURING THE VIEW AND IS NOT TRANSFERABLE

VISITORS

> A day with the York Tourist Society is generally one of unmingled pleasure, inasmuch as the most romantic scenery and the historical relics of bygone ages are visited, thus making us the better able to understand and appreciate the manners and mode of life of our Saxon and Norman forefathers, in the time of the royal Alfred and William the Conqueror, and through the transition period when the opposing races at last amalgamated as one people.[25]

Like many similar societies, the York Tourist Society organised a series of excursions (most of them day-trips), not only to Yorkshire sites, but also to houses like Chatsworth, Clumber, Belvoir and Alnwick. Their outings were only made possible as a direct result of the expansion of the rail network, although even by the 1870s, a visit to Conisborough Castle and Roche Abbey on the Great Northern Express could be quite an adventure:

> About seven miles from Doncaster ... we came to a sudden halt. Here all was excitement, as fears were entertained some sad disaster had befallen the slow train in advance of us, which left York about half an hour before ours. After waiting disconsolately for forty minutes, news at last came that its engine had broken down, and the express was ordered to push it on to Doncaster. Proceeding carefully, we ... were soon on the Doncaster platform, where an immediate rush was made to the refreshment room for the homeopathic doses for which the YTS are so famous.[26]

There was an element of antiquarianism in such expeditions, but it was not the dry, solemn antiquarianism of an earlier age: day-trips were fun. The members of the society were, as its name suggests, tourists rather than scholars, and were quite capable of distinguishing between the two occupations.

One obvious effect of the organised excursion – whether it made use of scheduled services or employed a specially chartered train, and whether it was run by a society or as a commercial venture – was the dramatic increase in the number of visitors which some of the larger country houses experienced. Newstead allowed a maximum of six visitors at any one time; but at Chatsworth, for example, the opening of the Midland Railway from Derby in 1849 meant that around 80,000 tourists were coming to the house each summer, a number that increased still further when the line reached Manchester in 1863. The first 'pleasure trip' to make use of the new Amber Gate and Rowsley line in 1849 consisted of a party of 500 'respectable, orderly and well-dressed individuals,' who, at 9 a.m. one Wednesday morning in June, arrived at Rowsley station, three miles away from Chatsworth.[27] Omnibuses, coaches and carriages stood waiting to carry the party – at a cost of sixpence a head – to the house, where the tourists were admitted in groups of twenty at a time, with a few minutes' interval between each tour. There was no admission charge, and the Duke of Devonshire's servants were apparently ordered not to demand or accept tips.

That the sixth Duke of Devonshire allowed such a large-scale pleasure trip to

Chatsworth is a good example of the expression of that sense of responsibility which the Victorian landowner was encouraged to cultivate, as the local newspaper was quick to point out: 'The playing fountains and flowing cascades in all directions gave indisputable proof that none felt more happy or more anxious than the noble Duke himself did in dispensing so much happiness to others.'[28] The Duke was displaying that *noblesse oblige* which, under pressure from an increasingly powerful middle class, the aristocracy was being encouraged to adopt. Nevertheless, such a display confirmed and strengthened his status, as the deferential tone of the newspaper also emphasised:

> Such an instance of condescension is perhaps without a parallel, and that which gave additional effect to the whole was, that all this took place while His Grace was at Chatsworth . . .
>
> During the admission of the visitors to Chatsworth His Grace was observed by some of the parties promenading on the grounds, and about two o'clock he took an airing in his carriage. This, to many, was the crowning gratification, for to see the noble Duke as well as Chatsworth, on one and the same day, was to consummate their happiness, and render that a day never to be forgotten.[29]

As the country houses became more accessible to the new middle- and artisan-class tourists, publishers were quick to cater for the demand for interpretive material to help them to appreciate their architecture and art. These guides were of three main types. At one level there were the books of description, accounts of the author's own experiences, such as Howitt's *Visits to Remarkable Places*, already mentioned in connection with Hampton Court. These blends of personal reminiscence, history, description and, occasionally, polemic were successors to the vast numbers of travel journals that appeared at the end of the eighteenth century and gradually petered out during the first thirty years of the nineteenth. Many of them functioned as essentially armchair guides, strong on atmosphere and weak on detailed information:

> The domestic offices on the ground floor [of Haddon Hall, Derbyshire] were extremely rude and uncouth in their appointments; such a buttery, kitchen, pantry, and cellarage are nowhere else to be seen, and might have been contrived for the use of a band of scathless banditti. Enormous beams to suspend the slaughtered ox, gigantic chopping blocks, a monarch oaken mincing board, worn through with long service . . . I could have wished for a peep into former days, for the bluff quaint figures assembled here in office, garbed in their leathern doublets and coarse habiliments, now obsolete to all remembrance, with their rough jokes and still rougher usages.[30]

Romantic association still figures strongly in such accounts, perhaps partly because the eighteenth-century interest in modern domestic architecture had largely vanished by the middle of the nineteenth century. It was the 'mansions of

England in the olden time' which drew the crowds, rather than the new Gothic Revival work of Blore, Burges and Scott. Indeed, Romantic association grew stronger as the century progressed, and not even a writer of the stature of Henry James was immune to it. When he visited Haddon Hall in 1877, and was shown the door through which Dorothy Vernon was said to have eloped with the young Sir John Manners in Elizabethan times, he was, temporarily at least, overcome:

> As I stood in the luminous dusk weaving the romance of the spot, I recognised the inevitability of a Dorothy Vernon and quite understood a Lord John. It was of course on just such an evening that the romantic event came off, and by listening with the proper credulity, I might surely hear on the flags of the castle court ghostly footfalls and feel in their movement the old heartbeats.[31]

But the spell did not last: 'The only footfall I can consciously swear to, however, is the far from spectral tread of the damsel who led me through the mansion.'[32]

This sort of architecture-inspired material served to set the scene for the reader who intended to visit a property, to prompt a visit and to act as a souvenir, a reminder of a tourist's experience. The second type of guide material was more practical. It usually took the form of a compendium of suggested itineraries, with rail links, together with more detailed architectural descriptions and practical information about admission charges and opening hours, since 'it is a surpassing annoyance to make a holiday . . . and then, after a journey perhaps of thirty miles or more, to be told you have selected the wrong day, and be denied admission'.[33] Such companions describe a whole range of houses and other attractions in a given area, sometimes only a county, sometimes nationwide. A late Victorian *Handbook for Derby, Notts, Leicester and Stafford*, for example, includes a 'Pedestrian Tour in Derbyshire of a Fortnight', which begins at Ashbourne station, and suggests visits to the Manifold Valley, Dove Dale, Chatsworth, Haddon Hall, Buxton, South Wingfield Hall, Hardwick Hall and Bolsover Castle.

Charles Knight's *Excursion-Train Companion*, on the other hand, covers the whole country, and in its descriptions of country houses contains a mixture of anecdote, fact and criticism. In the state apartments at Windsor, for example, would-be tourists are told that they will be 'waited upon by a man of intelligence, not to hurry [them] along, nor to disgust by his ignorant jargon, but to name the objects of curiosity, quietly and unobtrusively'.[34] But, if the attendant pleases, the presentation of the Castle itself is open to criticism: too few of the state apartments are open, the carpets are taken up and much of the furniture is hidden under brown-holland coverings. The rooms, seen under these circumstances 'have a very unstately appearance. It is like looking at a fair lady in curl-papers.'[35] In fact, 'most visitors acknowledge to feeling disappointment after going over them.'[36] And at Knole in Kent a Vandyke of Kenelm Digby, described as 'splendid' and worth a place in the National Gallery, 'ought not to be allowed to hang in its present wretched position'.[37]

fire-lock, a holster and pistols, a buff coat, and several pairs of jack-boots. One of the rooms in the Upper Court, under the Long Gallery, is styled, by Mr. Lysons, the Armoury.

At the north-west and north-east angles of the edifice are embattled towers, which give it the appearance of a castellated mansion. The lower entrance, as before stated, is through a gateway under the north-west tower. There is also another entrance into the Upper Court, a little on one side of the north-east tower. This, which is called the Eagle Tower, is furnished with an exploratory turret. The substructure of this portion of the building displays traces of higher antiquity than almost any other part, except the Chapel, and in both places probably we have the remains of the ancient castle of the Avenells.

This kind of literature is specifically designed to inform the visitor, showing a more discriminating, albeit less scholarly approach to the country house among the new tourists. Deference may still have been due to the nobility and gentry for allowing access to their houses, but an unquestioning response to those homes and their contents was considered neither necessary nor appropriate.

Such a degree of freedom of comment was not permitted in the third category of interpretive material provided for the Victorian visitor, the traditional, site-specific guidebook. This was sold in nearby towns and villages, and could not afford to run down the neighbouring big house. That would be bad for business. These guides remained much more conventional in their treatment of a property, giving its opening times, and history, and briefly describing the contents of each

Haddon Hall is full of romantic historical associations, and it was these that drew visitors to the house in the nineteenth century. The guidebook, *Haddon Hall in the Olden Time*, published in 1838, takes full advantage of this, as in this illustration of a medieval knight.

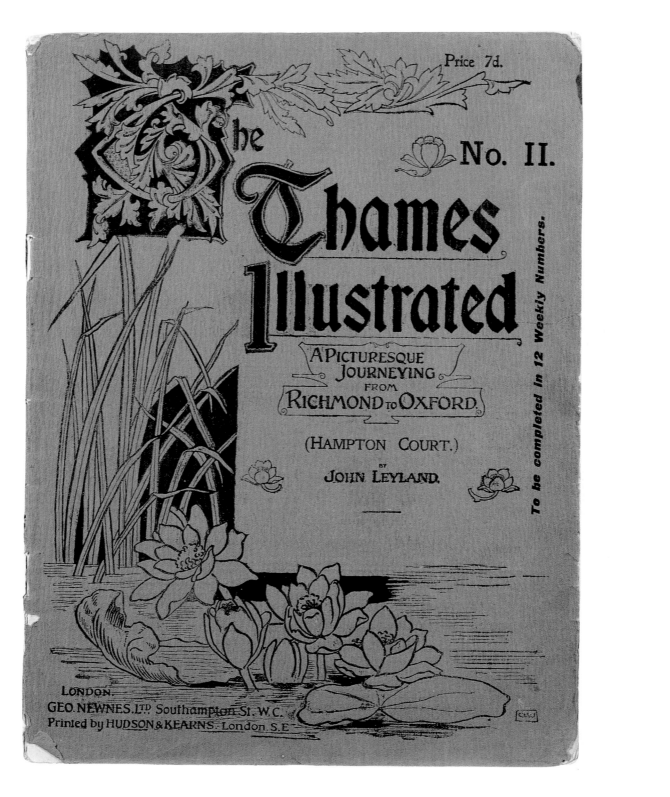

Price 7d.

No. II.

The Thames Illustrated

A Picturesque Journeying from Richmond to Oxford.

(HAMPTON COURT.)

BY
JOHN LEYLAND.

LONDON.
GEO. NEWNES. LTD. Southampton St. W.C.
Printed by HUDSON & KEARNS. London. S.E.

To be completed in 12 Weekly Numbers.

room. An extract from *Allen's Illustrated Guide to Alton Towers*, which dates from the 1870s, is typical of the genre:

> The OCTAGON, which is sometimes called the 'Sculpture Gallery', and the 'Saloon', is, as its name indicates, a room octagonal in plan, and is somewhat similar in design to the Chapter House of Wells Cathedral. A clustered column, of sixteen shafts, stands in the centre of this beautiful Gothic Chapel, from the floriated capital of which radiate the ribs of the vaulted roof. The ceiling is decorated with geometric tracery, pendant from which are pretty lanterns of Gothic design. The Octagon is lighted by lancet-shaped windows of stained glass, of rich colour and beautiful design. Under the principal window are two full-sized models of tombs of members of the Talbot family, one of whom was killed in 1453.[38]

The main interest of all such publications, in the context of country-house visiting, lies in the fact that large numbers were produced: the improvements in printing technology during the second half of the nineteenth century which led to cheap newspapers and popular literature also provided inexpensive paper-covered guides, illustrated and with maps, and usually costing no more than a penny or two.

What was the response of Victorian tourists to the country house to which they were being given access for the first time? According to Sir John Burke, genealogist and publisher of the *Peerage and Baronetage*, this varied according to social class. Writing in 1851, he noted that 'an interest of a very peculiar kind attaches to the Castles, Mansions, and Baronial Halls of England, of which every class in its own degree, and after its own fashion, is alike sensible'.[39] Attempting to analyse this appeal, he went on:

> With the uneducated, as a mass, this generally appears linked with the supernatural, or with deeds of violence and bloodshed; the man of imagination has the same feeling but under a higher and more fanciful aspect . . .
>
> The most republican disposition has a natural, and we may therefore infer a praiseworthy, curiosity, to become acquainted with the sites of great actions and the habits of illustrious characters. This kind of interest cannot fail to hang around most of our country Halls and mansions . . . No doubt, those in humbler situations do not always view with complacency the better fortunes of others; but with this, for the most part, mingles a vague feeling that the honour of their county is involved in the great men and noble seats that adorn it, and that that honour is in some manner their own. To all this must be added the beauty of the landscape in which our Halls and Mansions are placed . . . Those who are insensible to such considerations may, perhaps, find their imaginations more pleasantly stirred by the pictures, busts, relics, and curiosities, that almost ever abound in the Seats of our territorial proprietors.[40]

Excursion guidebooks became the vogue in the late nineteenth century. This special Hampton Court issue was published *c.*1898.

The various factors that Burke lists as accounting for the popularity of the country house – an interest in the more colourful episodes from its past, a desire to visit the spot where history was made, a local or national pride, an appreciation of landscape and an art-historical interest in the contents – seem to cover the preoccupations of the bourgeois Victorian tourist; and, while he may not admit it, he would probably list them in that order. By and large, he was looking for atmosphere and anecdotal history, rather than serious architectural and art-historical information. He was essentially a reconstructionist, wallowing in Romantic association to a much greater extent than his Georgian predecessor, and with little interest in scholarly matters: 'On the table [at Penshurst] is a Sidney relic – Sir Philip's two-handed sword ... It is a rather curious example of this kind of sword, but that is a point for the antiquary.'[41] He was, in other words, a sightseer, and one should perhaps add to Burke's list an element of voyeurism. Perhaps for the first time in the history of country-house visiting, the Victorian visitor was motivated as much by a simple desire to see how his 'betters' lived as by an interest in his historical, architectural and artistic heritage.

CHAPTER 7

England My England!

England my England! But which is my England? The stately
homes of England make good photographs, and create the
illusion of a connexion with the Elizabethans. The handsome
old halls are there, from the days of Good Queen Anne and
Tom Jones. But smuts fall and blacken on the drab stucco,
that has long since ceased to be golden. And one by one, like
the stately homes, they were abandoned. Now they are being
pulled down...
    This is history. One England blots out another.
                    D. H. Lawrence, *Lady Chatterley's Lover*, 1930[1]

THE PERIOD between 1870 and 1940 saw a rapid and dramatic expansion in tourism of all kinds among all but the poorest classes, so that by the inter-war years, the tourist industry had become a well-established part of British social and economic life. One estimate of the income derived from foreign tourists staying in Great Britain in 1934 put forward a figure of £25.5 million, a significant contribution to the balance of trade in comparison with exports of woollen goods (£28.8 million in 1934) and coal (£31.8 million).[2] In the same year, the economist John Harry Jones commented on the rapid growth of leisure and recreation, in an article entitled 'Tourist Traffic and Employment':

> At the beginning of the present century ... those who were able to go every summer for a holiday extending over a fortnight or a month were regarded as extremely fortunate; those who are now unable to go for a holiday of at least a week are regarded as extremely unfortunate. Thirty years ago the week-end habit was confined to an extremely small proportion of relatively wealthy people; it is now common among comparatively poor people ... The travelling public is still increasing by leaps and bounds.[3]

Professor Jones went on to suggest that service industries connected with tourism had expanded correspondingly, to predict that this expansion would become a major source of employment and to advocate changes in the educational system (to allow families greater freedom of choice in the timing of their holidays), the creation by railway companies of brand-new purpose-built resorts and a large-scale programme of road improvements to cater for the increased demand.
    The spectacular success of Thomas Cook's business serves to illustrate the growing demand for organised leisure travel. Cook, the most famous tour operator

of them all, began in 1841 by laying on temperance outings from Leicester to Loughborough. By 1877 Cook and Son, who described themselves as 'Pioneers, Inaugurators, and Promoters of the principal systems of Tours established in Great Britain and Ireland, and on the Continent of Europe', were operating all over the world.

For the traveller who had neither the means nor the inclination for a steamboat cruise down the Nile or a trip to Jerusalem or Algiers, regular excursions to the West of England, Scotland and Ireland were arranged, 'with the view of encouraging pleasure travel, through districts of the richest natural scenery, and visits to health resorts of universal celebrity, with varied adaptations to constitutional requirements'. Holiday-makers could buy tickets at one of twenty offices and agencies nationwide, both for travel and for accommodation – Thomas Cook was one of the first tour operators to establish a system of pre-bought coupons which could be exchanged at nominated hotels for 'meat breakfast, dinner, plain tea, bed and attendance'.

In the wake of Cook and Son's work as 'Pioneers, Inaugurators, and Promoters', the railway excursion came to be regarded as one of the cheapest forms of holiday transport. Large numbers of late Victorians and Edwardians, whose fathers and grandfathers would never have dreamed of taking a holiday by the sea, descended on rapidly developing resorts, many of which were already acquiring reputations as popular venues for working-class outings. Coastal towns in Lancashire, Yorkshire and North Wales drew crowds from the mechanised textile industries of the north of England, and by the 1870s south coast resorts such as Margate, Ramsgate and parts of Brighton had become decidedly plebeian in the eyes of many of the middle class, who preferred Folkestone, Torquay or Bournemouth.

Country houses, castles and abbeys within reach of the new resorts were the targets for organised and casual day-excursions. Regular charabanc services were laid on during the peak holiday months of the summer, and visitors to Bournemouth in 1882, for example, were told that Corfe Castle, nineteen miles distant, 'affords an excellent day's "outing," whether they seek a simple inspection of the magnificent ruins, or combine with it a pleasant picnic'.[4] Organised architectural and antiquarian excursions to country houses and abbeys, of the sort promoted by the various tourist societies described in the previous chapter, continued, and the bicycle also helped to give access to the countryside and thus to country houses and monuments. But it was the advent of another means of transport, the motor car, that was to have a more radical effect on country-house visiting in the twentieth century.

The car was, from its origins at the end of the century until well into the 1950s, essentially a middle- and upper-class form of transport. From very early on in its history, it was advertised and marketed as a way for the town-dweller to discover the countryside. After the First World War came the production of cheaper models, increasing the number of cars in Britain from around 250,000 in 1919 to nearly 1.5 million in 1929, roughly one for every thirty people. Possession of a car

Corfe Castle rising out of a misty dawn. Corfe, with
its connections with the Royal House of Wessex and
grisly deeds by King John, was a favourite destination
for charabanc excursions from Bournemouth at the
end of the nineteenth century.

conferred a privileged freedom on its owners. No longer did they need to rely on organised outings, train timetables and cabs to get them to and from a particular site; now they could bowl along the country lanes, exploring picturesque out-of-the-way hamlets and manor houses, with much greater speed.

A weekend excursion away from the hustle and bustle of town was appealing to many, and guidebooks designed specifically for the motorist appeared in increasing numbers after 1900. The authors of the *Autocar Road Book* of 1910 succinctly summed up the objectives of much of the material directed specifically at motorists. They claimed that their guide provided information about 'scenery and the villages, castles, cathedrals, ancient manor-houses, and rural churches of the country for a sight of which, it may be presumed, most travellers in these days use the roads'. Their avowed aim was to give 'condensed information for the cultured tourist, to whom the scenery and the historical and literary associations of places make a strong appeal', and they promised:

> In these pages will be found not only all most outstanding places with which it behoves those who love their country to be acquainted, but also a very large proportion of those less-known hamlets and rural districts which, not yet *exploités*, should give the traveller who comes, delighted, to their unspoiled beauties, something of the thrilful experience of an explorer.[5]

Shades of E. F. Benson's *Mapp and Lucia*? Dunlop, whose 1925 *Guide to Great Britain* was printed on paper 'specially prepared for general use on the road, and ... not affected by damp', went to the lengths of operating a free touring service, supervised by a Fellow of the Royal Geographical Society, which offered itineraries giving 'the best roads for trouble-free tours, and the most interesting and picturesque routes'.[6] Dunlop's *Guide* also contained an 'annotated map of "The Old Country" which will specially appeal to Tourists from abroad' – an indication of the growth of the overseas market – 'In the case of American Shrines, brief notes are appended.'

However, these new tourists were seen as a very mixed blessing by their more conservative counterparts. 'The charm and poetry of the country walk are destroyed by motoring demons,' wrote one antiquarian in 1911, 'and the wayside cottage gardens, once the most attractive feature of the English landscape, are ruined.'[7] Many non-motoring tourists shared the mistrust of, and contempt for, car-users shown by T. W. H. Crosland in his Edwardian six-point guide to dealing with motorists in the countryside:

1 When you go out for a morning walk be careful to take with you a good supply of arnica, splints, and surgical bandages. They may come in useful in the not unlikely event of your being knocked down.

2 Always carry on your person a pocket-book and a number of ready sharpened pencils. These will be useful for taking the numbers of the cars which run over you.

3 When you see a motor coming towards you, jump into the nearest ditch at once. The whole of the road, sidewalk included, belongs prescriptively to the motorist.

4 In turning corners keep quite close to the hedge or wall. Otherwise you may be cut off unawares.

5 In the event of a motor running over either yourself or a member of your family, be most careful not to swear at the occupants of the car. It is impolite, and motorists are genteel people.

6 And if you succumb to your injuries, always remember that you are dying in a glorious cause, namely, for the pleasure of . . . wealthy brewers, swagger Members of Parliament, record breakers, company promoters, and their ill-bred wives, sisters, cousins and aunts.[8]

But the number of motor tourists increased steadily, and for those unable to afford their own Sunbeam, Morris Cowley or Austin 20, there were charabancs and motor coaches running organised excursions in competition with the railways. Trips to local tourist attractions in horse-drawn charabancs were a common feature of holidays by the sea from the 1880s onwards, and by 1910, an Eastbourne firm was running a six-day tour of North Wales using a 22-seater motor coach. This was so successful that the same firm followed it up with a 21-day tour to John o'Groats. Other operators followed suit: in June 1913, for example, a company called Worthing Motor Services had adopted the name Sussex Tourist Coaches, and was offering an extended tour of the West Country.[9] Coach firms also realised the value to the tourist of their regular services. By the 1930s London Transport was issuing a series of booklets giving itineraries for country walks in the Home Counties and making use of the Green Line coaches to get the rambler from central London to his starting point.

Mention of country walks leads naturally to a more prosaic, but equally popular, means of transporting the tourist to his destination during the period 1870–1940: hiking. The virtues of rambling as a manly pursuit were extolled by many late Victorians and Edwardians. To men like W. H. Hudson, G. K. Chesterton and Hilaire Belloc, there seemed to be something peculiarly English about taking to the open road, and travelogues with titles like *Tramping in Yorkshire*, *Afoot in England* and *Rambles in Rural England* were available on most railway bookstalls. The craze for walking reached its peak during the inter-war years, when there were more than six hundred ramblers' clubs, with 50,000 members. Some indication of its popularity can be gauged by the success of the Youth Hostels Association (YHA), which was set up in 1931 to provide cheap accommodation for townspeople, most of them walkers, holidaying in the country. The YHA recorded 78,067 overnight stays in its hostels in 1931; by 1939 this had risen to 537,986.

England was on the move. By rail and bicycle, on foot, in cars and charabancs, people moved out into the country for day-trips, weekends and summer holidays, on a scale that had never been seen before. This inevitably had far-reaching effects on the country houses and castles, the ruined abbeys and ancient monuments which were often the targets for such excursions. Popularity brought with it a new set of problems and new grounds for criticism by the purist. Netley Abbey in Hampshire (admission twopence, sixpence on Sundays) had already been 'desecrated by being made into a place of popular junketings' by 1897. 'The garden is vulgarised by swings and such like; tea and other refreshments may be had; and' – most sinister of all – 'on moonlight nights the revellers are tempted to linger late.'[10] Poole's Cavern in Derbyshire was 'vulgarised by gas lighting' installed to cater for the large number of tourists visiting the Peak District from Manchester, Sheffield, Derby and Nottingham.[11]

Vandalism, while far from being a new problem, began to cause the owners of country houses and other architectural and archaeological sites serious concern. In 1913 the Hoare family at Stourhead felt compelled to publish the following notice:

> In consequence of wilful damage having been done by stone throwing to two of the Lead Statues in the Pleasure Grounds at Stourhead, the privileges which the public have enjoyed hitherto for nearly two hundred years have been reluctantly restricted.
>
> The same conditions for viewing will be imposed that were necessitated by the wilful misconduct of the public on three separate occasions at Alfred's Tower [also part of the Stourhead estate].
>
> For the future the Pleasure Grounds will be shown as hitherto to visitors on Mondays, Wednesdays, Thursdays, and Saturdays, between the hours of ten and six all the year round.
>
> Admission to the Grounds will have to be previously obtained by written or personal application at the Estate Office. Applicants must give their names and addresses, also state the number in party and make themselves responsible for same.[12]

Many owners took the same line as the Hoare family, by formalising visiting arrangements as a means of controlling access – and, incidentally, making a little money. Some reacted more forcefully, seeking to maintain – or regain – their privacy, by keeping their doors firmly closed in the face of an onslaught of holiday-makers. Haddon and Kedleston in Derbyshire were no longer open to the public, nor was Harewood in Yorkshire, or Woburn Abbey in Bedfordshire. But many more responded to the demand for recreational sites by establishing fixed visiting times and fixed admission charges. By the 1920s, well over 230 abbeys, castles, gardens and country houses in England alone – almost all pre-Victorian – were open to the public on a regular, fee-paying basis. For sixpence, the tourist could visit Little Moreton Hall ('teas provided'), or Beaulieu, or Corfe Castle, or Brighton Pavilion. A shilling would gain you admission to the state apartments at Windsor (although a sight of the Queen's Dolls' House would cost you another

THE TREASURER'S HOUSE

YORK BY L·N·E·R

ILLUSTRATED GUIDE FREE FROM TOWN CLERK OR ANY L·N·E·R OFFICE OR AGENCY

sixpence), Penshurst Place, or Studley Royal – refreshments at the lodge, lunch 2s 6d, tea 1s 6d; car-parking available, cycle 2d, motor car 6d. And some of the bigger houses could command even higher prices – Wilton, Knole, Warwick, Blenheim (state apartments open Tuesday, Wednesday and Thursday, 2–4, mid-May to mid-September; admission 2s, gardens 6d extra).

Profit was not the dominant force behind this widespread adoption of admission charges and regularised visiting hours. At Wilton, for example, where charges had been introduced by the late 1860s, annual income amounted to around £50 to begin with, dwindling to £20 or less within a few years – just over half the annual wage of a farm labourer. It was the desire to maintain social control in the face of a rapidly expanding demand which produced all those polite notices requesting sixpences, shillings and half-crowns. The tacit consensus about who was and who was not acceptable as a visitor, which had operated well into the nineteenth century, may have been in the process of breaking down completely,

Left: A photograph of the main street of Tintagel, Cornwall, taken by Francis Frith in 1894. The Old Post Office, a fourteenth-century hall house built in stone and slate, is on the left, with similar houses beyond. But the old buildings of Tintagel disappeared as hotels, cafés and boarding houses were built to cater for the tourists, drawn by the legends of King Arthur and Camelot. Today the Old Post Office (*above*) stands as an isolated reminder of the former village.

but the ability and inclination to pay for one's cultural entertainments could still work as an effective social sorting mechanism, while fixed hours allowed much more efficient forms of supervision.

The mere fact that more people *could* spend time and money visiting ancient manor houses, mansions, castles and other architectural sites is only half of the story of country-house visiting in the late nineteenth and early twentieth centuries. One still has to ask *why* so many tourists wanted to spend their leisure time exploring panelled halls and picturesque ruins. The answer lies in changing attitudes towards both the past and the countryside, and the country house as the embodiment of all that was best about both.

The 1851 census revealed that for the first time in the nation's history, those living in towns outnumbered their country cousins. By the end of the century, this imbalance had increased dramatically, and for the urban dweller, separated and perhaps alienated from rural life, the countryside became the expression of a whole set of values which were the antithesis of all that was negative about town life. The rejection of industrialisation and the dehumanising effects that it had on production workers and – via the poor aesthetic standards of mass-produced art-objects – consumers, which occupied thinkers and reformers like Thomas Carlyle, John Ruskin and William Morris, was readily transferred into a yearning for a non-industrial culture. This could be found in two places: in the past, and in the rural communities where pre-industrial values were thought, rather sentimentally, to survive. Stability, tranquillity, continuity and tradition were placed in clear opposition to what was seen as the moral and spiritual sterility of industrial England.

Such a dichotomy had its roots, of course, in Romantic thought: the superiority of nature over artifice, and thus of country over town, had become a cultural commonplace in the wake of much of the early nineteenth century's great literature. Keats wrote:

> To one who has been long in city pent,
> 'Tis very sweet to look into the fair
> And open face of heaven;[13]

and Coleridge, in 'Frost at Midnight', compared his upbringing in 'the great city', where he saw nothing of beauty but the sky and the stars, with his hopes for his child:

> But thou, my babe! shalt wander like a breeze
> By lakes and sandy shores, beneath the crags
> Of ancient mountain, and beneath the clouds.[14]

Looking down on Tintern Abbey during a tour in 1798, Wordsworth had declared himself 'A lover of the meadows and the woods, /And mountains'; a 'worshipper of Nature'.[15]

There were dissenters of course – William Hazlitt was of the opinion that 'There is nothing good to be had in the country, or, if there is, they will not let you have it',[16] rather as Sherlock Holmes was to remark to Watson a century later that 'the lowest and vilest alleys of London do not present a more dreadful record of sin than does the smiling and beautiful countryside'.[17] But the notion of the natural landscape as a positive force for moral good was a powerful and recurring theme in Romantic poetry, and to the middle-class artists and social commentators of the later nineteenth century the concept was given considerable reinforcement by what they perceived as the mechanistic, soul-destroying qualities which industrialisation had brought to urban man. The country, not only as landscape, but in the architecture that it contained, was purer, healthier, more organic, as Arts and Crafts architects like Baillie Scott were eager to point out: 'Those who dwell amidst the vulgar and impossible artistry of modern villadom may visit now and then some ancient village, and in the cottages and farmhouses there be conscious of a beauty which makes their own homes appear a trivial and frivolous affair.'[18]

Many of the English middle classes who spent their lives 'amidst the vulgar and impossible artistry of modern villadom' agreed with Baillie Scott's comparison. Modern, factory-produced architecture and design was very definitely out of fashion, and in the wake of Ruskin, Morris and the early Arts and Crafts Movement, anything that showed evidence of being handmade – buildings or furnishings – was in demand. Even new housing followed the trend, giving rise to a profusion of mock-Tudor and pseudo-vernacular villas erected in the main for the upper-middle classes.

Old was best, and the more quaint and weather-beaten your house, your garage or your wireless set looked, the better. This taste for old-world charm reinforced the expansion of tourism during the first decades of the twentieth century. The royal palace, which had interested the Elizabethan visitor, and the brand-new neo-classical mansion, which had struck the Georgian excursionist as an expression of culture and civilised living, gave way to the rambling manor house of the late Middle Ages as an archetype of all that was best about the nation.

T. W. H. Crosland's 1906 satire, *The Country Life*, poked fun at the prevailing attitude, while at the same time confirming its popularity. When town-dwellers find that the country is not all that it is cracked up to be (as they inevitably must), they set their unhappiness down to a defect in their own moral composition:

> Let [them] take heart ... Life in the country is not really either simple or elemental, and life in an agricultural community, or in the half-savage communities called villages, is no more natural than is life in the slums of the darkest cities. If it is not natural to live in tenement houses, it is certainly not natural to live in damp, ant-eaten, mosquito-haunted country cottages ... If it is desirable to live among pleasant and cultivated people, then again the country must be eschewed, because pleasant and cultivated people are even scarcer there than they are in the towns.[19]

But if Crosland's *Country Life* tried to debunk the myth of rural England, another, more famous *Country Life* reinforced the image. Edward Hudson's magazine first appeared in 1897, and was aimed from the outset at city-dwellers who yearned to experience the joys of the country. In its pages, the country house was portrayed as being at the core of country living, and at the same time a means of escape into a fictional past. The very first issue carried (beneath a piece on 'HRH The Princess of Wales's Pet Dogs') an article on the medieval Baddesley Clinton in Warwickshire, which contained the basic elements of an approach to 'olde Englande' that would be an integral part of middle-class attitudes towards the country house for decades to come:

> Among all the counties of Great Britain there are few shires more famous for princely mansions and quaint old houses of long-lineaged English gentlemen than that of Warwick. Standing amid great elms, in which for generations countless rooks have been accustomed to make their homes, they lift their many-windowed walls and battlements over old-world gardens to end in high gables and twisted chimneys, where doves flutter and coo in the sunshine. Mailed knights have dwelt within their walls, fugitives in troublous times have fled to their secret chambers, cavaliers have knocked at their oaken doors.[20]

This is the vocabulary of creative fancy with a vengeance: the deliberate archaisms – 'dwelt', 'troublous', 'oaken' – combine with knights in armour and secret hiding-places to produce an attractively vague, sanitised picture of the past as evoked by, and embodied in, the English country house.

But, more than this, values of stability and continuity – in opposition to what were perceived as 'modern' ideas of progress and change – were constantly impressed upon the reader. The country house was becoming the flagship of conservatism, and age as a positive virtue recurs over and over again, not only in the pages of *Country Life*, but wherever one looks in the literature:

> Age only mellows and improves our ancient houses. Solidly built of good materials, the golden stain of time only adds to their beauties. The vines have clothed their walls and the green lawns about them have grown smoother and thicker, and the passing of the centuries has served but to tone them down and bring them into closer harmony with nature. With their garden walls and hedges they almost seem to have grown in their places as did the great trees that stand near by. They have nothing of the uneasy look of the parvenu about them. They have an air of dignified repose; the spirit of ancient peace seems to rest upon them and their beautiful surroundings.[21]

This extract comes from a piece written in 1915 concerning the contrast between old mansions and contemporary 'suburban abominations'. The same sentiments – an affirmation of tradition, historic architecture as being somehow more in touch

with nature – could, and did, appear in countless similar works. 'One of the charms of old homes', wrote the owner of the medieval Ightham Mote in Kent in his 1909 account of the property, 'is that within their walls are enshrined memories and traditions of bye-gone days. The first question usually put regarding any old house is, "What are its historical connections?"'[22]

Popular perceptions had become fixed on the past and, in particular, on the 'olden times' of the late Middle Ages and the sixteenth and early seventeenth centuries. The *Country Life* article on Baddesley Clinton in Warwickshire explicitly

The moated manor house of Baddesley Clinton. This photograph appeared alongside an article about Baddesley in the first issue of *Country Life*, January 1897.

praises the house because its 'aspect carries you back hundreds of years', enabling you to 'conjure up an old-world history when you look at it' and to 'forget for the time that you are living in the Nineteenth Century'. The words 'old', 'old-world' and 'olden' appear ten times on a single page, and even the rooks have been around for generations. The furniture is old, or oaken (another image of solidity, age and pre-industrial Englishness); the portraits are old, and 'in the mind's eye dead men loom out of the shadows when the moonlight falls through the tinted glass'; there are even 'old inhabitants ... ever ready to hold forth on the traditions of long byegone tragedies enacted hard by'. These tragedies are at the core of a brief history of the house, providing the reader with details of three bloody murders and a resident ghost, and the piece finishes with a romantic reiteration of Baddesley's character, which is, of course, 'old-world': 'Swans glide gracefully upon that [moat] which still remains, gay flowers bestud the trim parterres, and modern elegance has added a new unobtrusive charm to a truly quaint and beautiful domestic survival of the English country life of the olden time.'[23]

The series of articles on 'Country Homes' soon became more scholarly and antiquarian, as *Country Life* enlisted the services of H. Avray Tipping in the years before the Great War, and Christopher Hussey in the 1920s and 1930s. But while John Leyland, the author of the Baddesley Clinton piece, may have been guilty of indulging an unhistorical imagination, he was nevertheless doing nothing more than expressing widely held attitudes towards architecture, attitudes that determined the tourist's response to the country house right up to the Second World War and beyond. Baddesley, or Knole, or Little Moreton Hall, or any of the old manors and palaces on display to the public, had become emblems of nationhood.

And, as early twentieth-century tourists, more mobile and independent than their predecessors, and at the same time much more remote from the occupants of the country houses that they visited, travelled through the countryside in search of old England, their quest was given an added intensity, their discoveries an extra significance, by the growing awareness that the England they valued so much was vanishing before their eyes.

By the turn of the century the natural rural landscape and those open spaces that survived in towns were being ably defended against insensitive development by a growing number of amenity societies – evidence of a recognition that their loss would be irrevocable. One of the earliest of these pressure groups, the Commons Preservation Society, had been formed in 1866 by George Shaw-Lefevre with support from Thomas Hughes, barrister and author of *Tom Brown's Schooldays*. Its aim was to fight for statutory public access to common land. From 1868 its honorary solicitor was Robert Hunter, who was later to be one of the founders of the National Trust.

The urban landscape had as its protector the Kyrle Society, an organisation dedicated to 'the diffusion of beauty' set up in 1878 by the housing reformer Octavia Hill – another founder of the National Trust – and her sister Miranda.

They proposed to do all in their power to beautify poor working-class districts of London, fighting for the provision of open spaces in the heart of the city, 'open air sitting-rooms for the poor', as Octavia called them, and even putting forward the idea of painting brightly coloured slogans on blank walls to liven up the dreary streets. Octavia Hill herself proposed that graffiti in the form of Charles Kingsley's injunction to 'Do noble deeds' should decorate a wall near Waterloo Station.

At first sight, these societies seem to have little to do with the late Victorian or Edwardian bourgeois tourist, guidebook in hand, marvelling over Tudor carvings

The romanticisation of the medieval country house reached new heights at the turn of the century. Sir Thomas Colyer-Fergusson, owner of Ightham Mote, wrote in 1909 that one of the charms of such places was that 'within their walls are enshrined memories and traditions of bye-gone days'.

The Founders of the National Trust.
Right: Octavia Hill. *Above, left to
right*: Benny Horne, who became
solicitor to the Trust, Sir Robert
Hunter, his daughter Winnie, and
Canon Hardwicke Rawnsley,
photographed out walking in the
Lake District, *c.*1900.

at Little Moreton Hall or the baroque murals at Chatsworth. But the desire to provide the poor with access to beauty grew out of the same attitudes that sent the white-collar worker in search of 'England in the olden times'. Indeed, those same tourists who spent their free time revelling, uncritically but affectionately, in the historical connections of Ightham Mote might also ramble over Romney Marsh or take a walking holiday in the Lake District.

The link between landscape and architecture in the middle-class imagination was perfectly expressed by Robert Hunter in a lecture on 'The Preservation of Places of Interest or Beauty' given at Manchester University in January 1907:

> In a very real sense, there is a similarity of feeling at the root of the interest felt by the antiquarian and the lover of nature. Both desire to perpetuate something which is apart from the life of the present, something which, on the one hand, speaks of the continuity of the human race, and on the other of the slowly acting giant forces of nature.[24]

The 'desire to perpetuate' which Hunter noted also provided a further bond between unspoilt scenery and historic buildings: both were threatened.

Fears that the new would swamp the old were hardly a modern innovation; concern over the disappearance of the 'venerable mansions of antiquity' had been routinely voiced by the Georgians. But the railways that took the modern tourist out into the countryside also disfigured it. And the developer who sold the mock-Tudor villa might have demolished a Queen Anne country house and swept away its gardens in order to build it – and its fifty identical companions. The improved standard of living that tourists now enjoyed, the result of cheap imports from abroad, brought with it the great agricultural depressions of the 1870s, and the break-up of many of the big estates. The insensitive 'restoration-work' carried out on such pre-industrial buildings as remained destroyed that most prized quality, their 'old-world charm'. And if England was summed up for these tourists by the oak-beamed hall of a medieval manor house or the ivy-clad walls of a building put

Above: Stonehenge, Britain's most famous ancient monument, attracted large numbers of sightseers by the end of the nineteenth century. This photograph *c.*1895 shows visitors arriving by bicycle, charabanc and carriage to view the stones.

Alarmed at the potential damage of so many visitors, the Commons Preservation Society sought to place Stonehenge under the protection of the Ancient Monuments Act of 1882, but the owner of the site, Sir Edmund Antrobus, was determined to maintain his proprietorial rights. *Punch*'s contribution to the debate came in this cartoon in 1899 (*right*).

up for some courtier in the days of Good Queen Bess, then there was a sense in which that manor house, or that Elizabethan mansion, belonged to them. They may have felt alienated, separated from their roots; they may not have questioned exactly what their England consisted of, as Connie Chatterley did in the passage that opened this chapter; but they were sure that somehow, something that they owned, however indefinably, was being taken away. It was common property, part of their England, part of their heritage, and when it was threatened, they felt they had a right to say, 'Stop. You can't do that. That belongs to all of us.'

William Gilpin had been one of the first to declare that a piece of architecture was 'a deposit of which [the owner] is only the guardian, for the amusement and advantage of posterity'.[25] William Howitt had taken the process one stage further, by demanding that the public should have access, as of right, to royal palaces like Hampton Court. A third William, William Morris, initiated perhaps the first nationwide pressure group – as distinct from the dedicated amateur antiquaries who had been exerting pressure, both private and public, at local level for decades – devoted to preserving buildings for the enjoyment of all. In 1874 Morris had protested publicly against the demolition of part of Hampstead parish church. In September 1876, during a drive from his house at Kelmscott to Broadway in the Cotswolds, he caught sight of Burford Church being pulled down, an experience that, according to his daughter May, 'set my father to making notes for a letter of appeal for some united action'. The next spring a visit to Tewkesbury, where George Gilbert Scott was restoring – or in Morris's words, 'destroying' – the abbey, finally spurred the artist to write to the *Athenaeum*:

Is it altogether too late to do something to save it – it and whatever else of

beautiful or historical is still left us on the sites of the ancient buildings we were once so famous for? Would it not be some use once for all, and with the least possibly delay, to set on foot an association for the purposes of watching over and protecting these relics, which, scanty as they are now become, are still wonderful treasures, all the more priceless in this age of the world, when the newly-invented study of living history is the chief joy of so many of our lives?[26]

The first annual meeting of the 'association for the purposes of watching over and protecting these relics', the Society for the Protection of Ancient Buildings (SPAB), was held on 21 June 1878, with Morris as its secretary, and Thomas Carlyle, Sir John Lubbock, William Holman Hunt and Edward Burne-Jones among its committee members. 'Anti-Scrape', as the SPAB became known, from its opposition to the practice of scraping weathered stonework to make it smooth and characterless, initially concentrated its efforts on the preservation of ecclesiastical buildings, and Morris travelled the country, lecturing on the importance of keeping medieval architecture intact, and arguing with, persuading and occasionally offering physical violence to the clergy responsible for commissioning insensitive restoration work.

The formation of the SPAB marked a milestone in the history of the conception of a commonly held national architectural heritage. The idea that the nation had a collective responsibility for the preservation of certain elements in the built environment, and a right to enjoy them in their original state, is implicit in the notion of a pressure group like Anti-Scrape. Moreover, it also meant that society's view of those elements had moved one step closer towards overriding the

Right: The Clergy House, a fifteenth-century timber-framed building standing on the village green at Alfriston. It was the first building to be acquired by the National Trust, bought from the Ecclesiastical Commisioners for £10 in 1896. Badly dilapidated, its conservation was begun immediately with the guidance of the Society for the Protection of Ancient Buildings. This photograph (*above*) taken by Francis Frith shows the thatched roof already under repair.

individual's rights of ownership in favour of the collective good.

By the last decades of the nineteenth century, the government was itself taking halting steps towards protecting certain categories of important architectural and archaeological property. Four years before Morris's letter to the *Athenaeum*, Sir John Lubbock (later Lord Avebury) who was to be a founding member of the SPAB, and who was instrumental in giving working people more free time by pushing through the Bank Holidays Act (1871) and the Shop Hours Act (1889), first introduced into Parliament a bill for the protection of monuments. Nine years went by before George Shaw-Lefevre, as First Commissioner of Works, persuaded Gladstone's government to pass it in a modified form as the first Ancient Monuments Protection Act.

The Act allowed for a restricted range of archaeological sites – earthworks, megalithic remains, stone circles and tumuli – to be placed on a schedule and, if the owner consented, to be put under the guardianship of the state, or of a local

authority. Its powers were purely permissive: there was no provision for the preservation of any monument, no matter how unique and valuable to the community, without the agreement of the owner, nor was it possible to order public access to a site against the owner's will. It became an offence, punishable by a £5 fine or one month's imprisonment with or without hard labour, for anyone to injure or deface a scheduled monument, but unless the owner had placed a site in the guardianship of the Commissioners of Works, he was exempt from this – he could do what he liked to his own property.

But the principle that the nation had some responsibility to protect important historic monuments was established, and the scope of the legislation was extended by a second Act in 1900 to include buildings of historic, traditional or artistic interest, provided that they were not 'occupied as a dwelling-place by any person other than a person employed as a caretaker thereof, and his family'.[27] This last clause obviously excluded inhabited country houses, although County Councils, as opposed to the Commissioners of Works, could – and occasionally did – take on habitable buildings. By 1907 the Commissioners had scheduled eighty-six monuments in Great Britain and Ireland, including Silbury Hill, Cadbury Castle, Long Meg and her Daughters (the stone circle near Penrith) and Stonehenge, the country's most famous tourist attraction outside London, which had been fenced by its owners, and a charge made for admission.

Between the passing of the first Ancient Monuments Protection Act and the extension of its powers by the second, another force for the preservation of historic sites had come into existence. In 1884, in a lecture given to the National Association for the Promotion of Social Science in Birmingham, Robert Hunter of the Commons Preservation Society had advocated the formation of a 'Land Company' which could buy and hold land and buildings for the benefit of the nation as a whole. Over the next nine years, the idea developed of a body that would exist to do just that – to own and protect pieces of beautiful countryside or important and threatened historic buildings, thus ensuring their continued existence. Reactions were largely favourable: *The Times*, commenting on the first meeting of interested parties in November 1893, pronounced the scheme to be 'highly commendable from a public point of view', and suggested that the new association 'might seek powers of compulsory purchase in cases where the public interest is clearly involved'.[28]

Largely due to the efforts of Hunter, Octavia Hill and Hardwicke Rawnsley, who had been an active campaigner for the preservation of the Lake District against the depredations of railway companies, this 'Land Company' finally and officially came into existence as the National Trust for Places of Historic Interest or Natural Beauty on 12 January 1895. Not surprisingly, considering the interests of its founders, the Trust concentrated in its early years on the acquisition of open spaces, although by its tenth birthday it was caring for six historic buildings, including the Clergy House at Alfriston in Sussex (the Trust's first architectural property, a derelict pre-Reformation priest's house bought for £10 and restored by public subscription), the Tudor Joiners' Hall in Salisbury and the fourteenth-century Old Post Office at Tintagel.

Octavia Hill had, in fact, proposed in 1894 that the new body should take steps to preserve not only ruins and landscapes, but also more substantial buildings such as manor houses. However, the prospect of taking on something as large as a country house, with its park, gardens and estate, to protect it for the public good, was quite daunting. And in any case, the 'stately homes of England', important symbols of a disappearing world though they may have become by the twentieth century, were hardly in need of the care and concern of a body like the National Trust. Or so it seemed at the time.

CHAPTER 8

The Stately Home Business

[Everard Radcliffe of Rudding Park] has what may seem a
good old-fashioned attitude towards the public, though I
think many owners would sympathise with his opinion of the
greatest disadvantage of opening: 'The very special horrid
smell left in the house afterwards'.

Lord Montagu of Beaulieu, *The Gilt and the Gingerbread*, 1967[1]

IN NOVEMBER 1945, four months after the general election which brought
Clement Attlee's Labour government to power, *Country Life* ran a series of articles
on 'The Future of Great Country Houses'. The contributors, all country-house
owners, viewed the prospect of life in Attlee's Britain with alarm. They were
worried by the changes that were striking at their role in society and the fiscal poli-
cies that threatened their incomes. Their tone was defensive, self-justificatory and
massively sensitive to criticisms of privilege and inherited wealth. Privilege in
1945, declared Burghley's Marchioness of Exeter, means public service. Christopher Hussey, of Scotney Castle in Kent, was anxious 'for the electorate to disabuse
itself of the common confusion between a great historic house and housing'.[2]

The common link between all the articles was the conviction that action was
needed to ensure the continued existence of the country house. Only one of the
four contributors, H. D. Walston, saw change of use as a viable option. He
suggested that the key to the survival of smaller houses was for their owners to take
over their management personally, running them as working agricultural estates
and training centres, with the gardens converted into community recreation
grounds where villagers could look after and enjoy 'tennis courts, a cricket ground,
a bowling green, outdoor meetings of the Women's Institute on summer evenings
and similar activities'.[3]

The other three writers were reluctant to see their houses and gardens
converted into community centres and agricultural colleges. 'By what means shall
they be preserved?' asked the Marchioness of Exeter. 'As national institutions or
museums, or public schools and hospitals; or as living, warm family homes in
which every picture, or tapestry or piece of furniture has a story to tell?'[4] Like her,
Christopher Hussey and the fourth contributor, Lord Methuen, owner of
Corsham Court in Wiltshire, saw the future in terms of enabling owners to maintain their country houses as private homes. Financial aid from the state was the
answer: perhaps along French lines, according to which the government contributed

The Battle of the Fireplaces. Tattershall Castle in Lincolnshire was built in the 1430s and 1440s by Ralph, 1st Lord Cromwell, Treasurer to Henry VI. One of the features of his brick tower was the carved stone fireplaces, displaying the purse of his office (*above right*).

At the beginning of the twentieth century the castle, now in ruins, was sold to speculators who were said to be intent on dismantling it stone by stone and shipping it to America. The chimneypieces were ripped out and carted off to London. Lord Curzon, former Viceroy of India and leading Conservative statesman, was also a passionate conserver of historic buildings. He bought Tattershall in 1911, repaired the castle and recovered the chimneypieces from 'an obscure yard behind a London public house'. These photographs show them being returned in triumph to Tattershall, draped in the Union Jack, in June 1912 (*above*), while Curzon waits to receive them (*right*).

50 per cent towards the cost of essential maintenance, or in the form of manpower provided by the state to help to run the house, or as concessions from the Inland Revenue or a derating policy by local authorities.

But why? Why should a socialist government intervene to help an impoverished aristocracy? Why should funds be diverted from reconstruction at a time when 4.5 million British homes had been damaged or destroyed as a result of six years of war, when sterling debts amounted to more than £3,500 million, when, in Churchill's famous phrase, Britain was in a 'melancholy financial position'? What could the stately homes offer in return?

The answer was simple – public access. Preservation was in the interests of education, of the arts, of the crafts and of sociological development, as the Marchioness of Exeter put it. The immediate task and desire of owners, she wrote, was to reopen their houses to the public – if only they could find the staff. The other writers supported the concept of this trade-off, public funds in return for public access. In exchange for state aid, owners must agree to open their doors for a minimum of thirty-six days a year, declared Lord Methuen. The country house is Britain's unique contribution to tourism worldwide, said Christopher Hussey. Nowhere else is 'the conception of the "home" found with such richness and humanity of content, or with such endless variety, in harmony with the fine arts and the cognate arts of gardening, landscape architecture, and husbandry'.[5] In other words, if the country house had lost its place as a power-base for the ruling class, its role in post-war society was to be that of public museum in private ownership, a recreational and educational facility generating tourist income. A century after William Howitt had rejoiced that Hampton Court was, 'as it should be, given up to the use and refreshment of the people', country-house owners saw in those visitors' great-grandchildren a new *raison d'être*.

Clement Attlee's government was not the first to evoke fear and loathing in the owners of country houses. By the end of the First World War it already seemed to many that the country house would eventually cease to be a viable economic and social unit. Income tax, land tax and rates were together taking around 30 per cent of estate rentals, while the 1919 budget increased death duties to 40 per cent on estates of more than £2 million. Some owners sat tight and weathered the storm. Others rushed to sell. According to one estimate, between six and eight million acres, or one-quarter of England, was bought and sold between the end of the war and 1921. About half of the Duke of Rutland's Belvoir estate – 28,000 acres – went for £1.5 million, the Marquess of Ailesbury sold 25,000 acres of his Savernake estate in Wiltshire and 8,600 acres of the Marquess of Bath's Longleat holdings raised £350,000. And, inevitably, public perceptions of the landed classes were affected: 'England is changing hands', lamented *The Times*; 'The old order is doomed', wrote the Duke of Marlborough.[6]

In some cases, the house remained in the hands of the family, who retained perhaps the park and the home farm; in others, it was sold to a businessman, or converted into a school. But too often, it was simply demolished. Between 1918 and 1945, more than 450 country houses were destroyed in Britain, many of them of national importance. In Kent, for example, eleven important houses were deliberately demolished between the wars; Staffordshire lost twelve, two of which were the late Elizabethan Beaudesert Hall and Robert Smirke's Drayton Manor; and Lancashire thirteen, including the Tudor Agecroft Hall, which was re-erected in Richmond, Virginia in 1926. America was an important new market, not only for complete properties, but also for fireplaces and ceilings, staircases and overmantels, even whole rooms. When, in Alexander Korda's 1936 film *The Ghost Goes West*, a millionaire transports a Scottish castle to America, stone by stone, and finds that Robert Donat as the castle ghost has also made the transatlantic crossing, the kilted phantom may have been fantasy; the removal of an entire country house was most definitely not.

It is only in the context of this wholesale destruction that we can begin to make sense of the heated debate about the role of the country house which continues to this day. Quite apart from the self-interest that played its part in motivating country-house owners to mobilise opinion in their support, and which led them to portray themselves as beleaguered guardians of the nation's architectural heritage, the house had become a symbol of a more stable and secure set of cultural values; a symbol of a world that had already been lost. Now that symbol itself was threatened, and conservationists, antiquarians, art historians and country-house owners banded together to do battle with what they saw as the forces of progress and social change, the antithesis of everything the mansions of England stood for.

The result was a curious alliance of conservatives and radicals: a class whose privileged lifestyle was in danger coming together with the spiritual heirs of William Morris and Octavia Hill. The National Trust was the focus for much of this activity. It was a campaigning conservationist group, already established as a safe meeting ground between the two camps, which could number socialists and the nobility among its ranks, and which already held a number of historic buildings, although only two were country houses – Barrington Court and Montacute, both in Somerset. As a result of the great estate sales of the early 1920s, the Trust had already unsuccessfully lobbied the Chancellor of the Exchequer to give tax concessions to owners of historic buildings, to help with maintenance. In the 1930s it was urged to try again.

In July 1934, encouraged by the Trust's new Secretary D. M. Matheson, Philip Kerr, 11th Marquess of Lothian, gave a speech at the annual general meeting in the Inner Temple Hall in London. Lothian had been hit hard by death duties on inheriting his title and estates in 1930. In his speech he asked the Trust to 'extend its protecting arm in a more definite and considered manner than it had hitherto done over another part of our national treasure now threatened with potential destruction – the historic dwelling houses of this country'.[7] The main thrust of Lothian's argument was directed at the Treasury. He proposed that inhabited historic houses – which were still barred from being given into the care of the

Philip Kerr, 11th Marquess of Lothian. In his address to the Annual General Meeting of the National Trust in July 1934 he suggested that the 'country houses of Britain, with their gardens, their parks, their pictures, their furniture and their peculiar architectural charm, represent a treasure of quiet beauty which is not only specially characteristic, but quite unrivalled in any other land.' His own estate of Blickling (*overleaf*) must have been in his mind's eye when he made this speech, which paved the way for the introduction of the Country Houses Scheme.

Department of Works under the Ancient Monuments Acts – should be exempted from death duties unless they were sold; that the Treasury should allow all maintenance claims for sums spent on upkeep and restoration; that country houses could be exempt from death duties even if they were sold, providing that house, garden and contents were preserved as a whole, and provision made for public access from time to time; and that if these measures failed to preserve historic houses, then approved properties could be derated: 'Why should not the England of the future be full of public parks like that which surrounds Hampton Court, each with a historic house in its midst? If as a nation we had a scrap of imagination Parliament would be planning their preservation now.'[8] Finally, Lothian suggested that the National Trust itself should move to take on a number of furnished historic houses, a step that needed an Act of Parliament to allow the Trust, as a charity, to hold land or investments that would provide income for maintenance.

Lord Lothian's speech marked the beginning of a concerted campaign. His remarks were followed three months later by a similar call for action from W. Harding Thompson at the national conference of the Council for the Preservation of Rural England. Like Lothian, Thompson advocated a survey to establish which houses and parks were worth saving, and the setting up of an owners' association to lobby for the 'remission of duties in approved cases in exchange for regulated public access at specified times'.[9] The bargain that was to inform most post-war thinking about country-house tourism – rights of entry in exchange for cash benefits – had been offered, and numbers of conservationists and landowners began to press the Treasury for help.

At the outset, Lothian himself referred to the public's right of entry only in passing. He seems rather to have considered that the preservation, intact, of individual country houses – building, contents, park and family – was a good in itself; that they were part of the 'national treasure'. Following Thompson's speech, it was left to Matheson, in an announcement to the press inaugurating a new association of owners dedicated to securing tax advantages, to point out that 'no Government could face the loss involved in any remission of duties unless it could be shown that some real and considerable gain would accrue to the nation at large'.[10] Matheson realised that if some of the most privileged members of society wanted state aid to help them maintain their standard of living, they would have to give something in return; for them simply to exist, as a venerated British institution, was not enough.

The campaign that Matheson's announcement heralded was to be launched at a reception held by the Trust at the end of January 1936, and the projected lobby group that, it was hoped, would result, was to be modelled on the French *Demeure Historique*, part of whose programme stated that 'historic houses are social entities essential for the development of the tourist industry; and that they must be opened to the public'.[11]

This social compact between owner and tourist was a key factor in the campaign. Rights of access, far from being the minor consideration envisaged by Lothian, were the carrot which the new owners' association could dangle before the Treasury. Lord Zetland, the National Trust's Chairman, proposed that 'in return for an undertaking by owners to open their houses to sightseers ... the Government should be asked to make easier the upkeep and preservation of the houses by remitting some of the taxation that now burdens them'.[12]

In the event, lack of support from owners, and lack of encouragement from the government of the day, meant that Lord Zetland's proposal was stillborn. It was to be another thirty-seven years before this pressure group came into being as the Historic Houses Association, when one hundred owners came together with the declared aims of safeguarding their interests, lobbying to retain and maintain their homes 'in the interests of the Nation and the public at large'.[13] In the meantime, the Trust followed its own independent course. By October 1936 Parliament was being lobbied to pass a new National Trust Act, enabling the charity to accept a country house, its contents and estate, together with an endowment in the form of land or investments to pay for maintenance. In return, the owner and his or her descendants would be allowed to stay on in the house as tenants. A leader in *The Times* put the case for the Bill:

> The advantage to the owner combines freedom from responsibility with the assurance that the connexion of his family with the family seat shall not be sharply and completely broken. The advantage to the public combines freedom of access to treasures of natural and artistic beauty with the preservation of the character and occupation which makes the difference between a dwelling and a museum, a country place and a public playground.[14]

The new Act, which came into being on 1 July 1937, paved the way for the Country Houses Scheme, under which owners could give or bequeath their homes to the Trust. It was ironic that the first property to be acquired under the scheme was Sir Geoffrey Mander's Wightwick Manor in the West Midlands. With its Morris and Co. furnishings and its Pre-Raphaelite paintings, Wightwick was a masterpiece of the movement which had done so much to promote a sympathetic view of the country house as the epitome of old world charm. Yet in 1937 it had been standing for just half a century: it was only eight years older than the Trust itself, a far cry from the ancestral home sanctified by centuries of tradition which was perceived by many to be the epitome of the English country seat.

Other properties soon followed: Old Devonshire House in Bloomsbury, to be destroyed by German bombs in 1941, Lord Lothian's Jacobean Blickling Hall in Norfolk, Wallington in Northumberland, Cliveden in Buckinghamshire, Polesden Lacey in Surrey and Killerton in Devon. Throughout the war, owner after owner approached the Trust, whose Historic Buildings Secretary, James Lees-Milne, toured the country in a battered Austin, negotiating endowments and assessing the importance of individual properties. By 1945, the fiftieth anniversary of the founding of the National Trust, the charity owned seventeen houses, with restrictive covenants over five more. All of those seventeen were open to the public, and the interested visitor could enjoy a range of architectural splendours,

from the elaborate half-timbering at Little Moreton Hall in Cheshire and the medieval cloisters of Lacock Abbey in Wiltshire, to the clean neo-classicism of Robert Adam's Hatchlands in Surrey or Revett's portico at West Wycombe Park in Buckinghamshire.

Despite its new role as custodian and curator, the Trust made few positive steps to bring in tourists; in the decades following the war, conservation tended to take precedence over access (as it does today). While it was generally acknowledged that the opportunity for ordinary people – still perceived at this stage as middle-class amateurs rather than working-class sightseers – to gain direct experience of this element of their heritage was a primary reason for the country house's preservation, there was a certain ambivalence, both within the Trust and among the landed classes who were prepared to hand over their family homes. Looking back on those years, one has the impression that the preservation of the country house and the maintenance of the social hierarchy which it symbolised were the major objectives of many of those working for the Country Houses Scheme, that the protection of the status quo, regardless of society's changing needs, was an end in itself. Clough Williams-Ellis, himself one of the Trust's ablest and most sensitive supporters, confirmed that view in *On Trust For The Nation*, a survey of the Trust's holdings published in 1947:

> I have myself an instinctive, illogical and quite indefensible feeling that seemly architecture and a gracious landscape are sufficient ends in themselves, self-justified, regardless of their social implications, of the conditions that have produced them, or even of their own repercussions on humanity. That view, treating mankind as a mere foreground to inanimate beauty, as just figures in a landscape, cannot, I must own, be intellectually defended.[15]

Williams-Ellis was right. Such a view cannot be intellectually defended. However, the links between conservation and the public good were then in embryo, a subject for debate rather than an assumption underpinning action. The consequence was that for many, the visitor was a necessary evil, and not one to be actively encouraged.

Not every major country-house owner was in a position to present his or her property to the National Trust. Not every owner wanted to, either because they thought the Trust asked for too large an endowment or because they were not prepared to hand over a building which had been in their family's hands for centuries. Still in financial difficulties, they looked to other solutions which would allow them to retain ownership while at the same time finding fresh sources of income. True, the 1945 Labour government did not prove to be the iconoclast that many had feared. Hugh Dalton, Attlee's Chancellor of the Exchequer, created the National Land Fund out of the sale of surplus war-goods as a 'thank-offering for victory', enabling the Treasury to compensate the Inland Revenue for money lost

The Hall Alcove at Wightwick Manor, West Midlands. This Arts & Crafts house was the first to be acquired by the National Trust under the Country Houses Scheme in 1937.

by the transfer of houses to the National Trust in lieu of death duties. And in 1948, in an initiative that would lead to the opening up of a large number of mansions and manor houses, Sir Ernest Gowers was invited to chair a committee to examine the country-house problem. Various pressure groups and conservationist organisations, including the Society for the Protection of Ancient Buildings, the Georgian Group and the National Trust, made submissions to the committee, although no one seems to have considered the country house as a tourist amenity. Rather, the reasons which they put forward for preservation harked back to those of Victorian reformers like Morris, seeing the notion of an architectural heritage

The range of historic houses acquired by the National Trust as a result of the Country Houses Scheme is enormous – from medieval houses like Little Moreton Hall (*left*) to great baroque palaces such as Cliveden (*above*).

as a rather abstract good in itself, with little thought of how the public might be served by it:

> Like the men and women who occupy them, most buildings are relatively undistinguished; they have their day and are forgotten. But others, because of their architectural merits or their historical associations, have a value that extends beyond their own day; they become part of our national heritage, and form an essential link between the past and the present.[16]

Gowers's report, which appeared in 1950, concluded that because of changing social and economic conditions 'we are faced with a disaster comparable only to that which the country suffered by the Dissolution of the Monasteries'.[17] Some – although by no means all – of the Gowers Committee's recommendations for action were implemented by the Historic Buildings and Ancient Monuments Act of 1953, which allowed for the setting up in England, Wales and Scotland of Historic Buildings Councils. These councils were to advise their Secretaries of State about the listing and/or acquisition of buildings of outstanding historic or architectural interest or their contents or adjoining land, and about the awarding of grants and loans towards repair and maintenance, usually in exchange for an agreement by the owner to open his or her home to the public. It was this last provision that led many country-house owners to enter the tourist business over the next two decades.

These measures helped to ease the crisis somewhat, and advanced the notion that state aid must necessarily involve, if not public ownership, then at least a degree of public access to private homes. But it was not enough, and was, in any case, nothing more concrete than a good intention in the austere days of the late 1940s and early 1950s, when literally hundreds of houses were falling prey to death duties, desertion and developers. Yet in the context of that post-war austerity, the voyeurism that has always been an element in the tourist's response to the homes of the upper classes grew into a middle-class yearning for contact with a more opulent lifestyle. Just as the projected Festival of Britain was to be a 'corporate re-affirmation of faith in the nation's future',[18] the rediscovery of this aspect of our heritage was a re-affirmation of faith in the nation's past, and the remarks made by the Archbishop of Canterbury on the purpose of the Festival could apply equally to popular attitudes to the homes of the landed classes: 'It is good at a time like the present so to strengthen, and in part to recover, our hold on the abiding principles of all that is best in our national life.'[19]

Interest in the country house as escapist fantasy, first seen during the last decades of the nineteenth century, had been similarly heightened during the depression years of the 1930s, when it wasn't uncommon for annual visitor figures at major properties to reach fifteen, or even twenty thousand on a basis of thirty or thirty-six open days a year. The revenue from these tourists, at one or two shillings a head, almost invariably went to charity, after deductions for guides' wages. It would have raised more than a few eyebrows if the English nobility had been seen

"This is my last warning, Charles. If you do not mend your ways I shall leave the estate to you instead of to the National Trust"
H. F. Hoar "PUNCH" Jan. 22. 1947.

The Country House Problem, as the Chancellor of the Exchequer, Stafford Cripps called it, caused many owners to cast about for an escape from the burdens of responsibility for their estates. *Punch* came up with this cartoon for 22 January 1947.

to be pocketing the proceeds. Now everything was different, and the upper classes stood unashamedly – or occasionally, ashamedly – in need of cash. Perhaps one answer was to exploit the public demand for access, to turn the country house into a financially viable tourist operation.

The first to enter the stately-home business in any serious way was the sixth Marquess of Bath. In 1946 he inherited Longleat, an army of death-watch beetle and a bill for £700,000 in death duties. However, he also inherited the nearby Cheddar Caves, which had been opened to the public in the 1920s at a charge of one shilling per head per cave, and which had brought in 500,000 visitors a year – and 500,000 shillings. Desperate for funds to maintain his family home, the Marquess 'had the brainwave – why not open it like Cheddar Caves to the public?'.[20] On 1 April 1949 Longleat duly opened its doors to the public on a commercial basis: that is, to attract tourists deliberately and to see them as a means of financing the house. The Marquess stood on the steps to greet the first visitors, and guides were ready to conduct tours of the state rooms. 'We plumped for guides', he later recalled, 'because we thought Women's Institutes, British Legions, etc, like to be told funny anecdotes about the family. Quite frankly, I don't think that Rembrandts or Van Dycks interest them very much.' He went on to say, with disarming candour, that 'I'm not all that interested in pictures myself, although I love possessing them.'[21]

Visitors paid half a crown each. A guidebook, written by Lord Bath's wife, contained a history of the family, a family tree and nineteen pictures of the family, from Sir John Thynne, the Tudor builder of Longleat, to a portrait by Orpen of the fifth Marquess. In contrast, there were just eleven illustrations of the house inside and out. Lady Bath was perceptive enough to understand the appeal of the country house. Longleat was being visited, she wrote, 'as a thing of beauty in a drab and dreary world ... Let us hope that Longleat will really live again, not as a museum, but as Sir John Thynne, its builder, intended it to be – a home for the family.'[22]

With few rivals, and certainly none who deliberately sought tourists, Longleat, the 'Treasure House of the West', was an immediate success. Attendances were spectacular, totalling 138,000 in the first year. In 1952, Lord Montagu opened Beaulieu to the public; or, to be more accurate, he reopened it on a more commercial basis. The Abbey had been on show since the 1890s, and in 1950, the year before Montagu succeeded to the estate, 40,000 people had paid a shilling each to look round it. An experienced public relations man, he ushered in the new era with a shrewdly organised press campaign. Friends from Fleet Street were on hand during the weeks leading up to the opening, taking photographs of every stage of the preparations, including Montagu himself moving furniture, polishing the pewter and even scrubbing the floors. 'It's enough to bring a peer to his knees', declared a caption in the *Sunday Pictorial*. At a press preview, for which Montagu laid on a fleet of buses to ferry reporters and photographers in from the railway station at Southampton, he unveiled a surprise addition to the

The 6th Marquess of Bath with
Sheila Chipperfield and one of his
lions on the steps of Longleat in 1966.
The Times had frostily suggested that
'the proper place for lions, in an island
that is spared them, is in heraldry'.
But the Lions of Longleat proved
an irresistible draw for visitors.

Abbey – a motor museum, the first in England since World War One.

Three years later, another house entered the stately-home business. Faced, like Bath and Montagu, with colossal death duties on his succession in 1953, the 13th Duke of Bedford decided that the only way in which he could live in his ancestral seat of Woburn Abbey was 'to follow the tentative example of other families in our position, and allow the public to see it in return for an entrance fee'.[23] From the beginning, the Duke set out to present Woburn as a family home, in spite of the fact that his family lived elsewhere. His wife, he wrote a few years later, 'had succeeded most cleverly in arranging the main state-rooms for show while still making them look as if they were lived in'.[24] Bedford was not aiming at the student of art and architecture, but at the sightseer, the New Tourist with little art-historical knowledge, who responded more immediately to an anecdotal treatment of an aristocratic family than to a Velázquez, to displays of waxworks clothed in coronation robes rather than to the Sèvres china. Realising that he was one of the principal attractions, the Duke soon developed a routine of making a couple of tours of the house each afternoon, and doing a three-hour stint in the souvenir shop, during which time sales would regularly go up by between 30 and 50 per cent. His objective was quite simply to give the day-tripper a good time. Like Longleat and Beaulieu, Woburn was an instant success, drawing 181,000 visitors in the first year, 234,000 in the second and an awe-inspiring 37,000 on one single day, Whit Monday 1958. Most went away happy and one, at least, procured a new pet: the Duke's dog was carried off on the first day that Woburn opened, and never seen again.

It is a mark of the proficiency as self-publicists of Bedford, Montagu and Lord Bath that, looking back at the 1950s and 1960s, apart from the National Trust's properties, which were attracting relatively small numbers of tourists, it almost seems that Woburn, Beaulieu and Longleat were the only houses to open their doors to the public. The houses themselves, and more often their owners, made regular appearances on TV and radio and in the newspapers, as Montagu and Bedford in particular vied with each other to produce the most outrageous publicity stunt. A kaleidoscope of bizarre media images from those years yields a crash-helmeted Montagu go-karting at Beaulieu in company with DJ Pete Murray, or clinging to the top of a lamp-post while balancing on a penny farthing, or looking on helplessly while jazz fans riot during a live BBC broadcast from the fifth Beaulieu jazz festival. It yields the Duke of Bedford doing the twist with a sixteen-year-old on Australian TV, hosting a nudist camp at Woburn, playing the washboard with a skiffle group and offering his butler as a prize in an American competition. There is Bedford singing a duet with Lord Montagu on the BBC's *Tonight* programme (the performance consisted, inevitably, of Noel Coward's 'The Stately Homes of England') and the Marquess of Bath posing for a publicity shot announcing the 'Lions of Longleat', wearing a bandana and a cowboy hat, with a lion on a lead and the house in the background. 'Cattle, sheep and deer ought to be good enough for a Wiltshire man', roared an indignant *Times* leader.[25]

The stately-home business had become a *sine qua non* for self-advertising stunts, and the media lapped it up. Any publicity was good publicity: even the debate generated by its questionable taste only served to keep the country house in the public eye. The *Daily Telegraph* could ignore, in its 1966 league table of visitor figures, 'the limited number of stately homes with enormous totals from excessive showmanship'. In the same year Lord Antrim, the National Trust's Chairman, could disassociate the Trust from contemporary trends, announcing loftily that the organisation's job was 'not to involve itself in the entertainment industry'.[26] The public could look on, amused and bemused, sometimes with disapproval, more often with delight, at the spectacle of some of its most distinguished aristocrats conducting themselves in an uncharacteristically unaristocratic manner. But they still queued up to pay their half-crowns at the doors of country houses.

The 13th Duke of Bedford performing the twist at Woburn Abbey with a finalist in the 1962 National Dairy Princess Competition.

Other houses, many of which had been open to tourists since the day they were built, fell into line with contemporary commercial trends, even if their owners drew the line at jazz festivals and nudist camps. In fact, many had reopened fairly quickly after 1945 on much the same basis as they had in the 1920s and 1930s. Chatsworth and Blenheim, Hatfield House and Haddon Hall were all bringing in quite large numbers of tourists by the early 1950s. On Easter Monday 1952, for example, Blenheim welcomed more than four thousand visitors, and Chatsworth nearly six thousand.

But it was becoming difficult to ignore the additional attractions and souvenir shops which Longleat, Beaulieu and Woburn used to lure visitors through the turnstiles. Under varying degrees of financial pressure, owners made what Lord Montagu called 'the painful change from amateurism to professionalism',[27] making use of modern marketing techniques to sell an escape route from the brash commercialism of today's world. The tourist market was expanding dramatically: effective disposable income per head increased twofold between 1951 and 1970, paid holiday entitlement grew significantly and private car-ownership went from 2.2 million to 11.6 million.[28] There was money there to be made, and if it was unlikely to be enough to keep the traditional landed classes in the style to which their ancestors had become accustomed, it could at least make a valuable contribution to the upkeep of an expensive and inconvenient house.

By the early 1980s the country house had become a leisure industry, with condescension and class discrimination replaced by detailed analysis of spending patterns and demographic surveys. The tourist emerged triumphant, reversing traditional roles to the extent that whereas, in the past, the Thynnes of Longleat or the Dukes of Devonshire at Chatsworth could allow a few visitors to explore their homes as an act of *noblesse oblige*, by the end of the twentieth century the descendants of those polite tourists are courted and wooed as ardently as any government grant.

All of which is not to say that the country-house owner actually has to enjoy opening his family home to the public. The relationship between owner and visitor, which has grown more and more uneasy over the last two centuries with the gradual withering away of any consensus about social controls, has had to cope since the war with a wholly new factor – the tourist as necessary evil. The sightseer has become an essential element in a house's struggle to survive, and reactions to the situation have varied, from a cheerful acquiescence, such as that shown by Lord Bath – 'It isn't the same type of person that it was built for, but at least you feel they are enjoying themselves and you feel it is alive' – to a hypocritical contempt for the visiting public – 'The bulk of visitors in the holiday season are only here because they cannot think of anything better to do' – and a barely disguised resentment at having been forced to forgo one's privacy.[29]

Interest in the country house as a tourist destination has grown enormously since the war. By the 1990s, in excess of 1,300 historic buildings were open – more than 350 of them country houses – drawing well over 50 million visits every year. National Trust membership – a useful if imprecise indicator of the growth of public interest in historic houses – has grown from 7,850 in 1945 to 2.5 million in the 1990s. It might be an exaggeration to say that tourism has saved the country house after its mid-century crisis, but it has certainly helped.

On one level, the reasons for this dramatic increase in architectural tourism are straightforward enough: the population as a whole has more mobility and more leisure. But that tells us nothing about why, in the post-war years, the stately-home business should have grown into a multi-million pound industry. The mere fact that many more people *can* visit historic houses doesn't explain *why* they should want to spend so much time and money in doing so.

There is no single reason, of course. The presence of amenities, ranging from tea-rooms and souvenir shops to multi-media exhibitions, adventure playgrounds and miniature railways, are often as powerful a draw as the house itself. A 1982 University of Nottingham survey found that while only 9 per cent of visitors to six historic houses gave furniture and paintings as their most important reason for visiting – and only 7 per cent admitted to an interest in architecture – one in four simply said that they came for 'a day out' or out of general interest. However, the same survey found that more than half of those questioned said their main reason for visiting was to find out about 'how people lived in the past', a factor that had been highlighted back in 1949, when *The Times* applauded Lord Bath's decision to open Longleat to the public: 'As one of the great historic houses of England, now once again furnished as it was before 1914, it is likely to prove a "show-place" of very wide appeal, a memorial to a way and scale of living no longer possible.'[30]

The country house's appeal as a monument to a way of life 'no longer possible' has become its most potent attraction, although of course the reality is that like most historic houses, Longleat is a memorial to a way and scale of living which was *never* possible for most people. But that doesn't seem to worry us as we walk through the state rooms of Burghley or Blenheim, populating the great chambers and halls with earls of our own creation, interested not in the Claudes or the Chippendale, but in the lifestyle of those who lived there. Where are the kitchens? Where did the servants sleep? Is there a nursery? Our forebears' search for anything rare, anything strange and curious, has been replaced by an equally ardent search for the mundane and everyday.

Except, of course, that it isn't mundane. Time lends enchantment, even to a kitchen sink. The National Trust's pioneering experiments with the presentation of life below stairs at Erddig near Wrexham, which began when the Trust opened the restored house to the public in 1977, marked a genuine departure from the traditional focus on architecture, furniture and family portraits. The Yorkes, who had owned Erddig for 240 years, took an unusual interest in their domestic staff, commissioning portraits and later photographs of indoor and outdoor servants and even composing little doggerel verses extolling their virtues. The presence in the house of this unique collection, coupled with the survival of many of the estate workshops, led to the Trust's decision to present visitors with a more rounded view of the country house than had been seen before. This was itself a sign of a changing social order, of course: in the days when most country-house visitors had servants of their own, the below-stairs workings of a great house were about as interesting as watching paint dry. Instead of being welcomed at the front door at Erddig, visitors enter the house through the estate yard, stableyard and laundry, viewing the kitchens and servants' hall before making the transition to the state rooms above stairs.

Other houses have followed Erddig's example, at least to the extent of opening up their domestic offices and making them an integral part of a tour. At Lanhydrock in Cornwall, for example, the huge Victorian kitchen quarters, with their larders, sculleries, dairy and bake-house, help to attract around 140,000 visitors a year. In the fully equipped Tudor kitchens at Hampton Court, refurbished in the early 1990s, the visitor can now gaze with wonder – and perhaps some distaste – at rows of stuffed deer, rabbits and game-birds suspended from hooks in the Flesh Larder or draped artistically over tables and chopping blocks in the Boiling House butchery.

Entertaining and educational though the Hampton Court kitchens undoubtedly are, their stuffed animals and reproduction knives, cauldrons and tables inevitably raise the difficult question of authenticity. How legitimate is it to reconstruct the past in this way, and how 'real' is the experience without the searing heat of open fires, the hustle and bustle of servants, the noise and the smoke and the smells? Ultimately, the answer is probably not all that important, except to those whose business it is to develop and write about the presentation and interpretation of historic buildings. Of course it's not 'real', any more than the costumed guides in the state apartments at Hampton Court, who role-play courtiers from the time of Henry VIII or William III, are 'real'. But like their performance, the information and impressions offered by the Tudor kitchens are accurate and great fun. Where's the harm in that?

There is another issue, however. The Hampton Court kitchens take the visitor back to the 1530s when they catered for the huge court of Henry VIII. This act of restoration involved removing the remains of later grace-and-favour lodgings which had invaded the Tudor service block. It is not always so easy to strip away the accretions of centuries – nor is it necessarily a good idea. In the late 1980s a great deal of criticism was levelled at the decision to return the Queen's House at Greenwich back to the 1660s, when Henrietta Maria was living there after her years of exile during the Commonwealth. Sparkling new replica furniture and furnishings give the building a startling atmosphere, which is somehow at odds with our expectations of what an historic house should look like. The National Trust was faced with a similar situation at Sutton House, Hackney, once the London home of the Tudor courtier Sir Ralph Sadleir, but much altered over the centuries. Here, a different approach was adopted. Instead of stripping away the past, the Trust tried to show the various layers of the house's history by a kind of 'advent calendar' method, so that, for example, a section of the Georgian panelling can be lifted to reveal the Tudor fireplace beneath. Greenwich is much easier for the visitor to understand; Sutton House has perhaps retained rather more of its integrity.

The idea that a visitor's experience of a country house should be authentic has generated a great deal of debate in recent years, and the Trust, perhaps more than any other heritage organisation, has been involved in some intriguing experiments. In 1989 the Trust reopened Calke Abbey in Derbyshire, famously described in the media as 'a time capsule' and 'the house where time stood still', because the Harpur Crewe family, whose home it had been for 360 years, had kept everything – and redecorated nothing – since at least as far back as 1924. The decision was taken to preserve Calke as it was when the Trust acquired it in 1985, repairing but not restoring, stabilising structure and contents but making no

One of the remarkable series of portraits of servants hanging in the Servants' Hall at Erddig. This painting by John Walters in 1792, shows Edward Prince, the estate carpenter, with the house in the background. A verse by Philip Yorke II accompanies the picture, and tells us that Prince 'already had four Spouses; and if the present don't survive, hopes to rebuild them up, to five'.

One labour more, then muse of mirth
That broughtest dey.cl into birth
And before you leave us, enter
To record our old Carpenter.
'Tis threescore years, then young in graver
When here, at first, he held an hammer
Under his Father dead long since,
Who was entitled The black Prince.

A Raiser this indeed of Houses,
That has already had four spouses,
And if the Present, don't survive,
Hopes to rebuild them up to five:
From their bold strokes, arise a race
Of Princes, to adorn the place,
Who thrive beneath their parent stock,
And make good Chipps from that old block.

*I'm by the dancing
native styles of the
wine.

Ed.ᵈ Prince æt 73. 1792.

Old Charles Prince the present
Ed.ᵈ Father was the Carpenter,
it belong, in Mr Mellers time,
father was used to call him the
Black Prince, being a Welch again
dark Complexion'd Man.

attempt to return them to pristine condition. The process has recently been repeated at the early seventeenth-century Chastleton House in Oxfordshire, where a painstaking six-year programme of mending rather than restoring has left the building looking almost as gloriously dilapidated as it was when work began.

At Uppark, the Trust went to the opposite extreme. In 1989 a disastrous fire virtually destroyed the house, although prompt action by staff saved most of the contents. This time, the Trust determined that because the collection of furniture and art-objects which survived had been brought together *for the house* in the early eighteenth century, Uppark should be rebuilt in its entirety, even if the work amounted to not so much a restoration as a reproduction of the original. The cost of this came to a huge £21 million, paid out of insurance money that, to be fair, could only be used for reinstatement.

The decision provoked a great deal of criticism. To some, the idea of reconstructing a ruined house was a perfect example of the heritage industry gone mad, on a par with frequently aired proposals from English Heritage to build a publicly accessible reproduction of Stonehenge that would stand alongside the original. Criticism of the Trust's other ventures into authenticity has been just as marked. Calke has been derided as little more than a dowdy junk-shop; Erddig and Lanhydrock have been castigated for concentrating too much on below-stairs life. And those country houses where the emphasis remains firmly on the decoration and contents of the state apartments have been dismissed as elitist and out of touch with the modern world. A history book like this – and especially one published under the auspices of the National Trust – is scarcely an appropriate place to mount a defence against such criticisms, but one cannot help thinking that with so many attacks from so many different perspectives, the Trust must be doing something right.

In the midst of this plethora of interpretations – the costumed guides and piped period music, the time-capsules and mannered dilapidation, the dining-table carefully laid for a meal that will never be served and the rustic adventure playground in the park – one almost feels as though the country house, stone and glass and wood though it is, has no enduring, objective reality at all. The meaning that we attribute to Burghley or Kedleston Hall or Calke is conditioned by the cultural climate in which we live. Even if we saw precisely the same sights as the Elizabethan traveller, the Georgian excursionist or the Victorian rambler – the same house, the same rooms, the same pictures and furniture – we wouldn't see them in the same way. Our interpretation would be different, and it is that act that gives meaning to inanimate objects and spaces, the great staircases and the long galleries, the Rembrandts and the family portraits, the Sheraton and the Sèvres.

But we don't see the same sights. Montaigne was right when he said, 'We need to interpret interpretations more than to interpret things.' The most important thing to take away from the current debate on the presentation of the country house as a tourist attraction in the 1990s is that the meaning we attribute to what

The Fish Larder at Lanhydrock, part of the extensive service quarters provided for the house when it was rebuilt in the 1880s. The kitchens, dairy, larders and bakehouse have proved an enormous success with visitors.

we see is conditioned by factors external to the experience itself. Not only by our own ideological standpoint – whether we look back nostalgically to a mythical Golden Age when society was more stable and less threatening, or glory in the downfall of an effete and anachronistic ruling class – but by the people who do their best to mould our responses to what we see. They determine the route we follow. They select which paintings and furniture we shall see, and where we should see them. They write the guidebook we buy and design the publicity material that brings us to the house in the first place.

These presenters and interpreters determine the context in which we make our judgements about individual houses. Such is the competitive nature of the tourist industry that they try, within the constraints imposed by the needs of conservation, to give us what we want. So the dry-as-dust genealogies and saleroom catalogues of paintings and furniture are often supplemented with information that is more accessible and more interesting. These days, we are not only told when the dining-table at Uppark was made (in the late eighteenth century); we also learn that Emma Hamilton danced naked on it. If I had to hear one fact about that dining table, I know which one I'd choose.

But if we are not careful, the current preoccupation with life in the country house can deflect attention from the sheer beauty of what we see. We wonder how they keep the place clean, now that there aren't any servants to do the job for them. We ask about the kitchens, about life below stairs. We speculate over whether the amiable-looking old chap wandering round the garden is really the present Duke, and tell each other how awful it must be to have tourists invading one's home, as we queue for our timed tickets or sit in the tea-room leafing through the guidebook. And we think, perhaps a little guiltily, what fun it would be to live in a house like this.

Inevitably, cultural attitudes and assumptions are passed on to the tourist – through room layouts, through guide literature, through advertising material, even through the social backgrounds of the staff who show us round. And occasionally the process is more deliberate and more dishonest. Copies of *Punch* and *Country Life* are left with apparent nonchalance on the bedside table in a room which hasn't been slept in for decades, perhaps even centuries, a 'reminder' that the country house is still a home – even when it isn't. Guides are always ready with little anecdotes of the recent family birthday party, which always seems to have been held 'in this very room, just the Saturday before last'. The guidebook, which claims to have been written by the owner himself, talks intimately, confidentially, of 'my favourite piece of furniture', or tells you that 'this is the room where my wife and I breakfast in the summer months', but is really produced by an anonymous publicity officer. All these devices seek to direct the tourist's perceptions of what he or she sees, to create a particular image of a family home which functions in much the same way that it always has – apart from the ropes and the signposts, the labels and the car-park and the souvenir shop.

We only need to worry about such things if we think the country house

The glorious confusion of Sir Vauncey Harpur Crewe's bedroom at Calke Abbey. The Harpur Crewes were known for their eccentric habits, including a marked disinclination to throw anything away. When the Trust took over the house in 1985, it was decided to repair, but not to tidy.

possesses some inner truth at its core, some unchanging historical reality which is masked or distorted by the process of interpretation. But history is not about truth; it is about us, here, now, and our ambivalent relationship with the past. The country house is a cluster of images, with as much to say about contemporary society as it has about what has gone before. To the sixteenth century, it talked about power; to the eighteenth, taste; and to the twentieth, nostalgia for a world we never lost because we never owned it.

'We possess nothing certainly except the past', says Charles Ryder as he wanders round the deserted Brideshead, in the course of a novel which has become a byword for country-house nostalgia. Ryder couldn't have been more wrong. There is nothing certain about our possession of the past. It changes, like the present. We mould our ideas of it according to our own lights, our own society. Thomas Platter and Celia Fiennes, John Byng and William Howitt – all took what they wanted, and what their culture would allow them to take, from their experiences of the country house. The same is true for the modern country-house visitor. Our vision of the past – and the present – is just as transient as theirs. And one thing we can say for certain about the future of country-house visiting is that the generations of Platters and Fienneses and Byngs and Howitts who follow us are sure to look back with interest, amusement and perhaps a little bewilderment on the strange preoccupations of the polite tourist in the late twentieth century.

The Long Gallery at Chastleton House, where the Trust has sought to retain the quiet, faded charm of the Jacobean interior.

Notes

Introduction:
The First Tourists

1 Liberate Roll 40 Henry III, quoted in Margaret Wood, *The English Medieval House* (Bracken Books, 1985), p.397.

2 Quoted in Sidney Heath, *In the Steps of the Pilgrims* (Rich and Cowan, 1953), p.275.

3 Erasmus, *Pilgrimage to St Mary of Walsingham and St Thomas of Canterbury*, tr. J. G. Nichols (1849), in Heath, *In the Steps of the Pilgrims*, pp.278–9.

Chapter 1:
Built For Envious Show

1 *The Diary of Baron Waldstein*, tr. G. W. Groos (Thames and Hudson, 1981), p.43.

2 Lawrence and Jeanne Stone, *An Open Elite?* (Oxford University Press, 1986), p.144.

3 Bacon, *Gesta Grayorum* (1594), in J. Spedding, *Letters and Life* (1861), vol.I, p.336.

4 William Camden, *Britannia* (1610), tr. P. Holland, quoted in Mark Girouard, *Hardwick Hall* (National Trust, 1996), p.13.

5 Quoted in E. St J. Brooks, *Sir Christopher Hatton* (1946), p.158.

6 Ibid., p.159.

7 Barnaby Rich, *Fare-Well to the Military Profession* (1581).

8 *CSP Scottish*, 1547–63, p.248.

9 T. Wright (ed.), *Queen Elizabeth and her Times* (1838), vol.II, p.98.

10 Brooks, *Sir Christopher Hatton*, p.158. (The god Momus unreasonably complained about everything.)

11 John Nichols, *The Progresses and Public Processions of Queen Elizabeth* (4 vols, 1788), vol.I, p.xix.

12 Ibid., vol.II, p.107.

13 Ibid., p.108.

14 Ibid., vol.I, p.xviii.

15 John Leland, *Laborious Journey* (1546).

16 Ibid.

17 John Leland, *Itinerary* (1710).

18 Ibid.

19 Ibid.

20 Edmund Spenser, *The Ruins of Time* (1591), ll.169–72, 174–5.

21 Ben Jonson, 'To William Camden', *Epigrams* (1616), ll.1–2, 7–9.

22 William Camden, *Britannia* (1800 edn), tr. R. Gough, vol.I, p.205.

23 *A True and Most Faithfull Narrative of the Bathing Excursion, which His Serene Highness Frederick, Duke of Würtemberg ... Made a Few Years Ago to the Far-Famed Kindomm of England* (Tübingen, 1602), in William Benchley Rye, *England as Seen by Foreigners in the Days of Elizabeth and James I* (John Russell Smith, 1865), p.3.

24 *Diary of Baron Waldstein*, p.181.

25 Rye, *England as Seen by Foreigners*, p.5.

26 *Thomas Platter's Travels in England 1599*, tr. Clare Williams (Jonathan Cape, 1937), p.149.

27 *Colloquia et Dictionariolum septem lingarum* (1589), in Rye, *England as Seen by Foreigners*, p.xxxiv.

28 Justus Zinzerling, *Itineris Anglici verbissima delineatio* (1616), in Rye, *England as Seen by Foreigners*, p.132.

29 'Diary of the Journey of Philip Julius, Duke of Stettin-Pomerania [then Pomerania-Wolgast], through England in the year 1602', ed. Gottfried von Bülow, *Transactions of the Royal Historical Society*, n.s. 6 (1892), pp.39–41.

30 Ibid., p.33.

31 Rye, *England as Seen by Foreigners*, p.133.

32 'Diary of the Journey of Philip Julius ...', p.11.

33 *Diary of Baron Waldstein*, p.37.

34 *A Relation of the Journey ... in Company with his Serene Highness the Duke Lewis Frederick of Würtemberg* (British Museum Add. MSS 20001, 1610), in Rye, *England as Seen by Foreigners*, p.61.

35 *Thomas Platter's Travels*, p.166.

36 'Journey through England and Scotland made by Lupold von Wedel in the years 1584 and 1585', tr. Gottfried von Bülow, *Transactions of the Royal Historical Society*, n.s. 9 (1895), pp.256, 257.

37 *Diary of Baron Waldstein*, p.79.

38 Ibid., p.73.

39 'Diary of the Journey of Philip Julius ...', p.52.

40 'Lupold von Wedel', p.231; *Thomas Platter's Travels*, p.172.

41 *Thomas Platter's Travels*, p.191, 200.

42 John Donne, 'Satire', iv.

43 *Diary of Baron Waldstein*, p.37; 'Diary of the Journey of Philip Julius ...', p.19; Rye, *England as Seen by Foreigners*, p.132.

44 Ibid., p.134.

45 *Thomas Platter's Travels*, p.159–63.

46 *Diary of Baron Waldstein*, p.155.

47 'Diary of the Journey of Philip Julius ...', p.31; Rye, *England as Seen by Foreigners*, p.44; *Diary of Baron Waldstein*, pp.81–3.

48 Henry Wotton, *The Elements of Architecture* (1624), pp.118–20.

49 *Thomas Platter's Travels*, p.223.

50 'Diary of the Journey of Philip Julius . . .', p.13; 'Lupold von Wedel', p.233.

51 Robert Laneham, *A Letter*, in Nichols, *Progresses and Public Processions*.

Chapter 2:
A Madness To Gaze At Trifles

1 Henry Peacham, prefixed to Thomas Coryate, *Coryat's Crudities* (1611), in William Brenchley Rye, *England as Seen by Foreigners in the Days of Elizabeth and James I* (John Russell Smith, 1865), pp.139–40.

2 Justus Zinzerling *Itineris Anglici verbissima delineatio* (1616), in Rye, *England as Seen by Foreigners*, p.134; Celia Fiennes, *The Journeys of Celia Fiennes* (Macdonald, 1983), p.307.

3 'Diary of the Journey of Philip Julius, Duke of Stettin-Pomerania [then Pomerania-Wolgast], through England in the year 1602', ed. Gottfried von Bülow, *Transactions of the Royal Historical Society*, n.s. 6 (1892), p.31.

4 *The Hardwick Hall Inventories of 1601*, ed. Lindsay Boynton (Furniture History Society, 1971), p.29.

5 *The Diary of Baron Waldstein*, tr. G. W. Groos (Thames and Hudson, 1981), p.43–5.

6 John Buxton, *Elizabethan Taste* (Macmillan, 1966), p.80.

7 D. Piper, 'Some portraits by Marcus Gheeraerts II and John de Critz reconsidered', *Proceedings of the Huguenot Society*, 20, 2 (1965), p.212.

8 'Journeys of John Ernest, Duke of Saxe-Weimar, 1613', in Rye, *England as Seen by Foreigners*, p.159–67.

9 Richard Haydocke, *A Tracte containing the Artes of curious Paintinge Carvinge and Building* (1598), p.14.

10 *Peacham's Compleat Gentleman*, 1634, ed. G. S. Gordon (1906), p.125.

11 John Evelyn, *Diary*, 12 August 1689.

12 *Hardwick Hall Inventories*, p.29.

13 Journey through England and Scotland made by Lupold von Wedel in the years 1584 and 1585', tr. Gottfried von Bülow, *Transactions of the Royal Historical Society*, n.s. 9 (1895), pp.235–6.

14 'Journeys of . . . Duke of Saxe-Weimar', in Rye, *England as Seen by Foreigners*, p.165.

15 *Thomas Platter's Travels*, p.171.

16 Ibid., p.171–3.

17 Ibid., p.173.

18 Arundel to William Trumbull, Berkshire County Record Office, Trumbull Alphabetical Correspondence, vol.2, item III.

19 *Peacham's Compleat Gentleman*, p.160–1.

20 *Works*, vol.III, p.294.

21 *Peacham's Compleat Gentleman*, pp.160–1.

22 Obadiah Walker, *Of Education, Especially of Young Gentlemen* (1699 edn), p.35.

23 Public Record Office, State Papers Domestic, Charles I, 4, 1625, pp.155–6.

24 John Evelyn, *Diary*, 17 September 1657.

25 Quoted in Arthur MacGregor, 'The cabinet of curiosities in seventeenth-century Britain', in Oliver Impey and Arthur MacGregor (eds), *The Origins of Museums* (Oxford University Press, 1985), p.150.

26 Thomas Shadwell, *Works*, vol.I, pp.340ff.

27 P.de Blainville, *A Diary of the Journey Though the North of England made by William and John Blathwayt of Dyrham Park in 1703*, ed. Nora Hardwick (privately printed, 1977), p.11.

28 Daniel Defoe, *A Tour Through England and Wales* (2 vols., J. M. Dent, n.d.), vol.II, pp.107–8.

Chapter 3:
Arbiters of Taste

1 Lines 408–9.

2 Celia Fiennes, *The Journey of Celia Fiennes* (Macdonald, 1983), p.19.

3 Ibid., pp.123, 132.

4 Ibid., p.56.

5 Ibid., p.121.

6 Ibid., p.200.

7 Ibid., p.201.

8 William Cole in Horace Walpole, *Correspondence*, ed. W.S. Lewis (42 vols, Oxford University Press, 1937–), vol.X, p.332.

9 Richard Graves in a verse addressed to William Shenstone, quoted in B. Sprague Allen, *Tides in English Taste* (2 vols, Pageant Books, 1958), vol.I, p.75.

10 Quoted in Lawrence and Jeanne Stone, *An Open Elite?* (Oxford University Press, 1986), p.244.

11 Daniel Defoe, *A Tour Through England and Wales* (2 vols, J. M. Dent, n.d. [1928]), vol.I, p.4.

12 Horace Walpole, *Journals of Visits to Country Seats &c*, ed. Paget Toynbee (Walpole Society, 1928), p.68.

13 Ibid., p.77.

14 Ibid., p.41.

15 Dr John Moore, *A View of Society and Manners in Italy* (1792), quoted in Christopher Hibbert, *The Grand Tour* (Spring Books, 1974), p.144.

16 Andrew W. Moore, *Norfolk and the Grand Tour* (Norfolk Museums Service, 1985), p.20.

17 Ibid., p.16.

18 Ibid., p.23.

19 Ibid., p.24.

20 Fiennes, *Journeys*, p.118.

21 Ibid., p.119.

22 James Plumptre, 'A Journal of a Tour into Derbyshire in the year 1793', Cambridge University Library MSS 5804, f.31.

23 Walpole, *Correspondence*, vol.X, p.314.

24 Henry Hoare to Susanna, Lady Bruce, 23 October 1762 (private collection); Walpole, *Correspondence*, vol.XXXV, p.149.

25 Anon, *Royal Magazine*, February 1764.

26 Mrs Philip Lybbe Powys, *Passages from the Diaries*, ed. E. J. Climenson (Longmans and Co., 1899), p.168.

27 Guy Miège, *The New State of England* (1691), pp.136, 244–5.

28 Defoe, *Tour*, vol.II, p.80.

29 Anthony à Wood, *Survey of the Antiquities of the City of Oxford*, quoted in Allen, *Tides in English Taste*, vol.II, p.51.

30 Thomas Gent, *The Ancient and Modern History of the Loyal Town of Ripon*, (1733), p.26.

31 Pocoke, *Travels*, vol.II, p.51.

32 Thomas Hearne, quoted in Allen, *Tides in English Taste*, vol.II, p.55.

33 Walpole, *Journals*, p.29; *Correspondence*, vol.XXXV, p.304, to Strafford on Hardwick, 4 September 1760; *Correspondence*, vol.IX, p.297.

34 *The Connoisseur* (1756), in Allen, *Tides in English Taste*, vol.I, p.110.

35 Walpole, *Journals*, p.26.

36 Alexander Pope, *Moral Essays*, Epistle IV 'To Richard Boyle, Earl of Burlington', ll.141–2, 145–6.

37 Ibid., ll.153–8.

38 Defoe, *Tour*, vol.II, pp.6, 8.

39 Pope 'To Richard Boyle', ll.179–80.

40 James Lees-Milne, *English Country Houses: Baroque* (Country Life, 1970), p.30

41 Edmund Burke, *A Philosophical Enquiry into the Origin of our Ideas of the Sublime and the Beautiful*, in *Works* (Bohn, 1854), vol.I, p.54.

42 Robert Harley, 'Journeys in England', Historical Manuscripts Commission Report, Portland MSS, VI (1901), p.161.

43 Lord Hervey, *Memoirs of the Reign of George II* (1884), vol.II, p.320.

44 James Cawthorn, *Of Taste* (1756).

45 Edmund Burke, *Correspondence* (10 vols, Cambridge University Press, –1978), vol.II, pp.394–5.

46 Burke *Philosophical Enquiry*, pp.90, 93.

47 Ibid., pp.141–2.

48 Ibid., pp 64, 67.

Chapter 4:
The Polite Tourist

1 Horace Walpole, *Correspondence*, ed. W. S. Lewis (42 vols, Oxford University Press, 1937–), vol.XXV, p.423.

2 Mrs Philip Lybbe Powys, *Passages from the Diaries*, ed. E. J. Climenson (Longmans and Co., 1899), pp.165–6.

3 Walpole, *Correspondence*, vol.XXXIX, p.40.

4 Mark Girouard, *Life in the English Country House* (Yale University Press, 1978), pp.189–90.

5 Quoted in R. W. Ketton-Cremer, *Norfolk Assembly* (Faber and Faber, 1957), pp.193–4.

6 Ibid., p.189.

7 Walpole, *Correspondence*, vol.XLII, p.275.

8 Robert Clutterbuck, 'Journal of a Tour through the Western Counties of England during the Summer of 1796', Cardiff Public Libraries MS 3.277.

9 John Byng, *The Torrington Diaries*, ed. C. Bruyn Andrews (4 vols, Methuen Library Reprints, 1970) vol.I, p.237.

10 Ibid., vol.I, p.231.

11 Richard Sulivan, *Observations Made During a Tour Through Parts of England, Scotland and Wales* (1780), p.143.

12 Walpole, *Correspondence*, vol.XLL, pp.219–20.

13 John Harris, 'English country house guides, 1740–1840', in John Summerson (ed.), *Concerning Architecture* (Allen Lane, 1968), p.63.

14 Byng, *Torrington Diaries*, vol.IV, p.135.

15 Walpole, *Correspondence*, vol.XXXIII, p.411.

16 Anonymous, 'Travel diary August–October 1761 and August–September 1762', British Museum Add. MS 27951.

17 Sulivan, *Observations*, p.142.

18 Anonymous, 'Journal of Tours in the Midland and Western Counties of England and Wales in 1794, and in Devonshire in 1803', British Museum Add. MS 30172.

19 William Bray, *Tour Through some of the Midland Counties, into Derbyshire and Yorkshire ... performed in 1777*, in *The British Tourist*, ed. William Mavor (6 vols, 2nd edn, 1800), vol.II, p.318.

20 Yorke MSS, in Esther Moir, *The Discovery of Britain* (Routledge and Kegan Paul, 1964), p.60.

21 Byng, *Torrington Diaries*, vol.II, p.44.

22 *Osterley Park* (HMSO, 1977), p.53.

23 Richard Warner, *A Tour Through the Northern Counties of England and the Borders of Scotland* (2 vols, 1802), vol.I, p.118.

24 Ibid., p.117.

25 Anonymous, 'A journal of a tour from Oxford thro' the Peak of Derbyshire, 1786', in *The Topographer*, 1 (1789), p.317.

26 Bray, *Tour Through some of the Midland Counties*, in *British Tourist*, ed. Mavor, vol.II, p.311.

27 Sulivan, *Observations*, p.144.

28 Bray, *Tour Through some of the Midland Counties*, in *British Tourist*, ed. Mavor, vol.II, p.311.

29 *Boswell's Life of Johnson*, ed. George Birkbeck Hill (6 vols, Clarendon Press, 1934), vol.III, p.161.

30 Warner, *Tour Through the Northern Counties*, vol.I, p.128.

31 Ibid., pp.120–1.

32 Sulivan, *Observations*, p.145.

33 Byng, *Torrington Diaries*, vol.I, p.53.

34 William MacRitchie, *Diary of a*

Tour Through Great Britain in 1795 (Elliot Stock, 1897), p.104.

35 Robert Clutterbuck, 'Journal of a Tour to the West of England from Salisbury, Wiltshire, 10 April 1801', Cardiff Public Libraries MS 4.367.

36 Warner, *Tour Through the Northern Counties*, vol.I, p.130.

37 Robert Clutterbuck, 'Journal of a Tour through the North of England & part of Scotland . . . during the Summer of 1795', Cardiff Public Libraries MS 3.277.

38 Thomas Pennant, *The Journey from Chester to London* (1783), p.347.

39 Warner, *Tour Through the Northern Counties*, vol.I, pp.124, 125–6.

40 Pennant, *Journey from Chester to London*, p.133.

Chapter 5:
Creative Fancy

1 William Combe, *Dr Syntax – His Three Tours in Search of the Picturesque, of Consolation, of a Wife* (Frederick Warne, n.d. [1871]), p.71.

2 William Gilpin, *Observations on the Western Parts of England, Relative Chiefly to Picturesque Beauty* (1798), p.328.

3 William Gilpin, 'On Picturesque Travel', in *Three Essays* (1792), pp.54–6.

4 Gilpin, *Observations on the Western Parts*, p.197.

5 Adam Walker, *Remarks Made in a Tour from London to the Lakes of Westmoreland and Cumberland, in the Summer of 1791* (n.d.), p.3.

6 The National Trust is at time of writing restoring Claife Station to its original state.

7 James Plumptre, *The Lakers* (1797), p.19.

8 Ibid., p.58.

9 Dr E. D. Clarke, *A Tour Through the South of England, Wales, and Part of Ireland, Made during the Summer of 1791* (1793), pp.189–90.

10 John Byng, *The Torrington Diaries*, ed. C. Bruyn Andrews (4 vols, Methuen Library Reprints, 1970), vol.III, p.74.

11 *The British Tourist*, ed. William Mavor (6 vols, 2nd edn, 1800), vol.I, p.vi.

12 Byng, *Torrington Diaries*, vol.II, p.39.

13 *The Topographer*, 1 (1789), p.iii.

14 Richard Cumberland, *The Fashionable Lover* (1772), Act II, scene ii.

15 Stebbing Shaw, 'Tour to the West of England in 1788' in *British Tourist*, ed. Mavor, vol.IV, p.248.

16 Byng, *Torrington Diaries*, vol.I, p.23.

17 Richard Sulivan, *Observations Made during a Tour Through Parts of England, Scotland and Wales* (1780), p.192.

18 Arthur Young, *A Six Months Tour Through the North of England* (1768), quoted in C. Hussey, *The Picturesque* (Frank Cass, 1967), p.195.

19 William Gilpin, *Observations . . . on the Mountains and Lakes of Cumberland and Westmoreland*, 1786 (Richmond Publishing, 1973), p.188.

20 Uvedale Price, *Essays on the Picturesque* (3 vols, 1810 edn), pp.52, 54.

21 Ibid., p.54.

22 Richard Warner, *A Tour Through the Northern Counties of England, and the Borders of Scotland* (2 vols, 1802), vol.I, pp.268–9.

23 Moy Thomas, 'Description of a Tour to the Isle of Wight & into the West of England in the Summer of the Year 1810', Bath Reference Library MS.

24 Thomas Wharton, *Pleasures of Melancholy, Poetical Works* (2 vols, 1802), vol.I, p.69.

25 *The Topographer*, 2 (1790), p.iii.

26 Anonymous description of Tynemouth Priory in *The Topographer*, I (1789), p.31.

27 Edmund Burke, *A Philosophical Enquiry into the Origin of our ideas of the Sublime and the Beautiful*, in *Works* (Bohn, 1854), vol.I, p.144.

28 Archibald Alison, *Essays on the Nature and Principles of Taste* (4th edn, 1815), pp.26–7.

29 Ibid., p.40.

30 William Bray, *Tour Through some of the Midland Counties, into Derbyshire and Yorkshire . . . performed in 1777*, in *British Tourist*, ed. Mavor, vol.II, p.298.

31 Ann Radcliffe, *A Journey Through Holland . . . to which are added Observations During a Tour to the Lakes* (1795), p.372.

32 William Howitt, *Visits to Remarkable Places* (Longman, Brown, Green and Longman, 1840), p.39.

33 'A Fellow of the Society of Antiquaries of Scotland', *Here and There* (John Russell Smith, 1871), pp.197–8.

34 Fanny Symonds, 'A Holiday in Cornwall 1836', Bodleian MS Don c 166, ff.245–8.

35 Byron, *Don Juan*, canto 13, stanzas 50, 55, 67.

36 Ibid., canto 13, stanza 59.

37 Thomas Bailey, *Handbook to Newstead Abbey* (W. F. Gibson, 1855), p.47.

38 Byron, *Don Juan*, canto 16, stanza 21.

39 *Allen's Popular Hand-Book to Newstead Abbey* (R. Allen and Son, n.d.), p.37.

40 S. J. Mann, 'Newstead in 1841', *Sketches and Reminiscences* (1856), p.41.

41 Quoted in Ian Jack, *English Literature 1815–1852* (Oxford University Press, 1963), p.42.

42 Thomas Frognall Dibdin, *A Bibliographical, Antiquarian and Picturesque Tour in the Northern Counties of England and in Scotland* (2 vols, 1838), vol.II, pp.1011–12.

43 A. W., 'A Few Notes, Scraps,

Remembrances &c of a Journey of Pleasure Taken by AW and JST', Bodleian MS Top gen f 35, ff.6a, 10a, 10a–10b.

44 Howitt, *Visits to Remarkable Places*, p.200.

45 Walter Scott, *Ivanhoe*, ed. A. N. Wilson (Penguin edn, 1984), p.79.

Chapter 6:
A Well-Pleased Throng of People

1 *The Times*, 7 December 1841.

2 Ibid.

3 *The Times*, 8 December 1841.

4 Ernest Law, *The History of Hampton Court Palace* (3 vols, George Bell and Sons, 1891), vol.III: *Orange and Guelph Times*, p.327.

5 Ibid., p.362.

6 William Howitt, *Visits to Remarkable Places* (Longman, Brown, Green and Longman, 1840), p.234.

7 William Gilpin, *Observations . . . on the Mountains and Lakes of Cumberland and Westmoreland*, 1786 (Richmond Publishing, 1973), p.188.

8 Howitt, *Visits to Remarkable Places*, p.235.

9 *Gentleman's Magazine* (May 1840), p.453.

10 Howitt, *Visits to Remarkable Places*, pp.236–7.

11 *The Times*, 2 November 1852.

12 *The Times*, 5 November 1852.

13 *The Times*, 20 November 1852.

14 Howitt, *Visits to Remarkable Places*, p.238.

15 Thomas Wright, 'Bill Banks's Day Out', in *The Savage Club Papers*, ed. A. Halliday (1868), p.223.

16 Ibid., pp.224–5.

17 E. Bulwer Lytton, *England and the English* (2 vols, 1833), vol.I, p.35.

18 W. Cooke Taylor, *Notes of a Tour in the Manufacturing Districts of Lancashire* (Manchester, 1842), p.132.

19 *Report of the Select Committee of Inquiry into Drunkenness among the Labouring Classes of the United Kingdom*, PP VIII (1834), p.viii.

20 Sir George Gilbert Scott, *Secular and Domestic Architecture* (1857), p.141.

21 A. W., 'A Few Notes, Scraps, Remembrances &c of a Journey of Pleasure Taken by AW and JST', Bodleian MS Top gen f 35, ff.7a–7b.

22 *The National Encyclopaedia* (14 vols, William Mackenzie, n.d.), vol, XI, p.343.

23 Charles Knight, *Knight's Excursion-Train Companion* (Charles Knight, 1851), p.iv.

24 *Allen's Popular Hand-Book to Newstead Abbey*, (R. Allen and Son, n.d.), p.4.

25 J. Brown, *Tourist Rambles in Yorkshire, Lincolnshire, Durham, Northumberland and Derbyshire* (Simpkin, Marshall and Co., 1878), p.35.

26 Ibid., pp.37–8.

27 'Excursion to Chatsworth by Rail from Derby, June 1849', quoted in the Duchess of Devonshire, *The House* (Macmillan, 1982), p.86.

28 Ibid., p.87.

29 Ibid., p.88

30 S. J. Mann, *Sketches and Reminiscences* (1856), pp.6–7.

31 Henry James, 'Lichfield and Warwick', *English Hours* (Oxford University Press, 1981), p.48.

32 Ibid.

33 Knight, *Excursion-Train Companion*, p.24.

34 Ibid., 'Windsor', p.8.

35 Ibid., p.10.

36 Ibid.

37 Ibid., 'Kent', p.20.

38 *Allen's Illustrated Guide to Alton Towers* (R. Allen and Son, n.d.), pp.6–7.

39 Sir John Burke, *A Visitation of the Seats and Arms of the Noblemen and Gentlemen of Great Britain* (1851), p.i.

40 Ibid., pp.i–ii.

41 Knight, *Excursion-Train Companion*, 'Kent', p.16.

Chapter 7:
England My England!

1 D. H. Lawrence, *Lady Chatterly's Lover* (Penguin edn, 1966), p.162.

2 *The Times*, 12 July 1935.

3 J. H. Jones, 'Tourist traffic and employment', *The Accountant* (1934), pp.354–5.

4 *A Descriptive Guide to Bournemouth, Christchurch, Wimborne and Corfe Castle and their Interesting Features* (T. J. Hankinson, 1882), p.93.

5 Charles G. Harper, *The Autocar Road Book* (Methuen, 1910), p.13.

6 *The Dunlop Guide to Great Britain* (E. J. Burrow, 2nd edn, 1925), p.945.

7 P. H. Ditchfield and Fred Roe, *Vanishing England* (Methuen, 1911), p.13.

8 T. W. H. Crosland, *The Country Life* (Greening, 1906), pp.98–100.

9 Gavin Booth, *The British Motor Bus* (Ian Allen, 1977), p.28.

10 A. R. Hope Moncrieff (ed.), *Black's Guide to Hampshire* (Adam and Charles Black, 13th edn, 1897), p.124.

11 Karl Baedeker, *Great Britain* (8th revised edn, 1927), p.294.

12 George Sweetman, *Guide to Stourhead* (Wincanton, 1913), p.28.

13 John Keats, 'Sonnet – To one who has been long in city pent . . .'.

14 Samuel Taylor Coleridge, 'Frost at Midnight' (1798).

15 William Wordsworth, 'Lines Composed a Few Miles Above Tintern Abbey' (1798).

16 William Hazlitt, 'Observations on Mr Wordsworth's *Excursion*'.

17 Arthur Conan Doyle, 'The Copper Beeches', *The Adventures of Sherlock Holmes* (1891).

18 M. H. Baillie Scott, *Houses and Gardens* (1906), p.1.

19 Crosland, *The Country Life*, pp.147–9.

20 John Leyland, 'Baddesley Clinton', *Country Life*, I, (1897) p.21.

21 Ditchfield and Roe, *Vanishing England*, pp.200–2.

22 Lady Hope, *English Homes and Villages* (1909), p.216.

23 Leyland, 'Baddesley Clinton', p.22.

24 Robert Hunter, *The Preservation of Places of Interest or Beauty*, (Manchester University Press, 1907), p.7.

25 William Gilpin, *Observations . . . on the Mountains and Lakes of Cumberland and Westmoreland*, 1786 (Richmond Publishing, 1973), p.188.

26 Quoted in Philip Henderson, *William Morris: His Life, Work and Friends* (Thames and Hudson, 1967), p.194.

27 Ancient Monuments Protection Act 1900 (63 & 64 Vict Ch 34, 1).

28 *The Times*, 17 November 1893.

Chapter 8:
The Stately Home Business

1 Lord Montagu of Beaulieu, *The Gilt and the Gingerbread* (Michael Joseph, 1967), p.120.

2 Christopher Hussey, 'Housemaids mean tourists', *Country Life*, 126 (1945), p.951.

3 H. D. Walston, 'The country house as a centre', *Country Life*, 126 (1945), p.905.

4 The Marchioness of Exeter, 'The future of great country houses', p.813.

5 Hussey, 'Housemaids mean tourists', p.950.

6 *The Times*, 19 May 1920, 22 March 1919.

7 Ibid., 20 July 1934.

8 Ibid.

9 Ibid., 29 October 1934.

10 Ibid., 8 January 1936.

11 Ibid.

12 Ibid., 26 February 1936.

13 John Cornforth, *Country Houses in Britain – Can They Survive?* (Country Life/British Tourist Authority, 1974), p.113.

14 *The Times*, 20 October 1936.

15 Clough Williams-Ellis, *On Trust for the Nation* (Paul Elek, 1947), p.18.

16 Nicholas Boulting, 'The preservation societies' in R. Strong, M. Binney and J. Harris (eds), *The Destruction of the Country House* (Thames and Hudson, 1974), p.175.

17 Quoted in Robert Hewison, *The Heritage Industry* (Methuen, 1987), p.62.

18 Festival of Britain *Exhibition of Science guide-catalogue* (HMSO, 1951), p.4.

19 Archbishop of Canterbury, 17 July 1950, quoted in *Festival of Britain – 1951* (HMSO, 1951), p.1

20 Montagu, *The Gilt and the Gingerbread*, p.104.

21 Ibid., pp.108, 109.

22 The Marchioness of Bath, *Longleat*, (Longleat Estate Co., 1949), p.53.

23 John, Duke of Bedford, *A Silver-plated Spoon* (Cassell, 1959), p.195.

24 Ibid., p.204.

25 *The Times*, 2 September 1965.

26 Montagu, *The Gilt and the Gingerbread*, p.90.

27 Ibid., p.10.

28 A. J. Burkart and S. Medlik, *Tourism* (Heinemann, 1974), pp.52, 53.

29 Montagu, *The Gilt and the Gingerbread*, pp.111, 129, 131.

30 *The Times*, 31 March 1949.

List of Plates

Index